CAT BREEDS
OF THE
WORLD

CAT BREEDS
OF THE
WORLD

A complete reference to cat breeds, characteristics
and showing your cat

Paddy Cutts

HERMES
HOUSE

This paperback edition published by Hermes House
an imprint of Anness Publishing Limited
Hermes House, 88-89 Blackfriars Road, London SE1 8HA

Published in the USA by Hermes House, Anness Publishing Inc.
27 West 20th Street, New York, NY 10011

Publisher: Joanna Lorenz
Senior Editor: Judith Simons
Editor: Lesley Ellis
Art Director: Peter Bridgewater
Designer: Annie Moss
Illustrator: Vana Haggerty
Production Controller: Joanna King

Printed and bound in Singapore

© Anness Publishing Limited 1993, 1999, 2001
Updated © 2002

3 5 7 9 10 8 6 4

CONTENTS

CAT BREED CLASSIFICATIONS

Although pedigree cats do not range in size to the same extent as pedigree dogs, there is still a tremendous selection to choose from. Breeds vary, not just in shape, colour and size, but in character and personality too. Some are far more demanding than others, some do not like to be left alone, others prefer to live in a quiet house. Do not be tempted to buy a kitten purely on its looks, or the fact that its colour suits your furnishings. No reputable breeder would sell you a kitten on those terms anyway.

Some cat breeds are old, derived from a natural selection, and may even be unique to a particular region. The tailless Manx cat is a good example of this. More recent pedigree breeds have been genetically engineered by breeders. By introducing new coat colours and patterns and different lengths of fur, breeders have made it possible to find pedigree cats in a kaleidoscopic range of colours.

Cat fancies around the world group pedigree cats in slightly different ways. Some breeds only exist in a few countries, while others are available worldwide. In this book, the pedigree section has been arranged roughly along the lines of the British Governing Council of the Cat Fancy (GCCF) registration system, but detailing alternative names of breeds, where applicable.

There are seven basic groups of cat, each outlined here, or eight if you include the most popular of all cats, the domestic moggie, or non-pedigree.

Longhairs, Persian Type

These all conform to the same standard of points for type, shape, size and length of fur. They all have short noses, little ears and an abundance of fur. They are available in a multitude of colours and patterns. In general, they are quiet, placid creatures that will not demand too much attention. Where they do need extra help is in their grooming; allow at least fifteen minutes a day. If you do not have this time to spare, do not contemplate a Persian cat, no matter how beautiful it may look.

Longhairs, Non-Persian Type

The only factor that these all have in common is the length of their fur. Each breed is unique, both in type and temperament. Within this group are Birmans, Turkish, Maine Coons and Norwegian Forest Cats, to name but a few. There can be no

BELOW
The Birman is one of the most popular of the non-Persian type of Longhair. This pair of Blue-points clearly show the typical restricted coat pattern and the white paws unique to this breed.

generalization as to their characters, as they all are different.

British and American Shorthairs

Like the Persian breeds, these all look basically the same, although there are some differences between the British and American standards. These tend to be quieter creatures than other shorthair varieties, but still need extra grooming because of their thick, short coats. They can grow to be very large and heavy, so if you prefer a small cat, look to one of the other groups.

Other Shorthair Breeds

These are grouped together for convenience. Some varieties, such as the Exotic Shorthair, are actually judged in the longhair section in the UK and there are some longhairs that come into this shorthair category for judging. The group includes all shorthaired cats that do not fit into any other designated shorthaired group. It is similar to the Longhaired Cats of Non-Persian Type section, in that the varieties are all different in appear-

RIGHT
For those who prefer a larger breed of cat, the British Shorthair is the answer. Although available in many colours and patterns, the Blue is probably the most popular.

ABOVE
Within the general classification of 'other shorthair varieties' are a myriad of breeds that do not fall into a specific group section. This Egyptian Mau is a spotted cat, but the type is quite distinct from the Oriental Spotted Tabby, a close relation.

ance and temperament. Included in this group are Abyssinians, Cornish and Devon Rex, American Wirehair and Curl, and the newer varieties such as the Asian cats, including Burmillas, and the spotted Bengals and Ocicats.

Oriental Shorthairs

These are cats of Siamese shape and size, and should conform to the Siamese standard of points. The difference is that they do not display the restricted coat pattern, genetically called the Himalayan factor. They come in a myriad of coat colours and patterns, but are essentially of Siamese temperament.

Burmese

Burmese are a very distinctive grouping, all of the same type and character; only the coat colours vary. They are active cats, need lots of attention, and do not like to be left on their own. In general, however, they are not quite as noisy as Siamese. They have such remarkable characters and loving dispositions that they are one of the most popular breeds of cat today.

Siamese

Siamese are very popular and relatively easily obtained. They are elegant, sleek, and have the most distinctive coat patterns. Like the Burmese, they do not simply need attention – they demand it.

The following chapter describes the details of all these breeds, their character, and the standards needed for a cat to be worthy of a show Challenge or Premier certificate in the UK, or their equivalents in America and Europe (*see Showing Your Cat*).

Before choosing a cat: remember that all cats are first and foremost family pets, so consider the time that each individual breed will require, both for grooming and attention. Your cat is going to be living with you for many years.

LEFT
Siamese are the most instantly recognizable breed of pedigree cat, and one of the most popular. Available in many different colours and patterns, this Blue-point epitomizes the elegance of this enchanting breed.

ABOVE LEFT
The Korat is one of the oldest-known natural breeds of blue cat, and originates from Thailand where it is considered to be 'Si Sawat' – a symbol of good luck. It is only seen in the original blue colour.

RIGHT
The first Burmese, a brown cat called Wong Mau, was imported into the USA in the 1930s. Today, Burmese are available in ten different colours all conforming to the basic standard of points as shown in this pretty young Cream.

Genetics

Genetics could be considered a science of probability, if a science can be thought of as based on the *possibility* of what could occur and not on precise, proven results. In the mid 1880s George Mendel, an Austrian monk, became increasingly fascinated by the different colours he found among the peas that grew in the monastery garden. He felt there must be some sort of divine order that decided which plants were of which colour and petal shape, which produced wrinkled or smooth peas, and even which were more dwarf-growing than others. What he was really looking at was the outward manifestation (or *phenotype*) of the genetic make-up (or *genotype*) of the plant; this was the beginning of what we now call genetics, which governs both the outward and inward appearance of every living thing – including cats.

Mendel discovered that by selectively pollinating plants with flowers of the same colour, the new plantlets' flowers were nearly always the same colour as the parents'. He continued his research to see if this were also true of animals. For this he selected tame mice, because they breed with great speed, and found again that if two similar parents mated together, the offspring tended to have the same colour as the parents.

However, when two pea plants of different colour, or mice of different coloured coats, produced offspring, the colour produced in the offspring appeared to be dominated by one or other of the parents. Things now started to get interesting: by breeding from two of the same first generation, some of the plants, or mice, resembled one parent and some the other. Mendel had discovered that there are two types of gene, one dominant and one recessive. He had also discovered that all living beings inherit one set of genes from each parent. So how does this basic information relate to cats?

COAT INHERITANCE PATTERN IN CATS

There are many different genes that make up a cat: those for the body, eye and head shape; those for colour, length, and pattern of coat; and even those which can carry a weakness towards certain defects. The combinations can be endless and so in this book I will explain, simply, the coat inheritance pattern.

The phenotype (outward appearance) is dictated by the genotype (genetic make-up), and with the fur of the cat there are three main areas of possibility: longhair or shorthair; differences in colour; differences in pattern.

Coat Colour

As a simple beginning, you could start with two Brown Burmese, both carrying the recessive blue gene. Mate the two together, and each kitten will receive one gene from each parent. The result should be what is commonly termed the Mendelian ratio of 1:2:1 – one brown kitten, two browns carrying the recessive (blue) gene, and one blue. The process is shown more simply in the diagram (*below*), where **D** represents the dominant brown gene and **d** the recessive blue.

This example considers only one set of 'characters', that of coat colour, and so is relatively simple to work out.

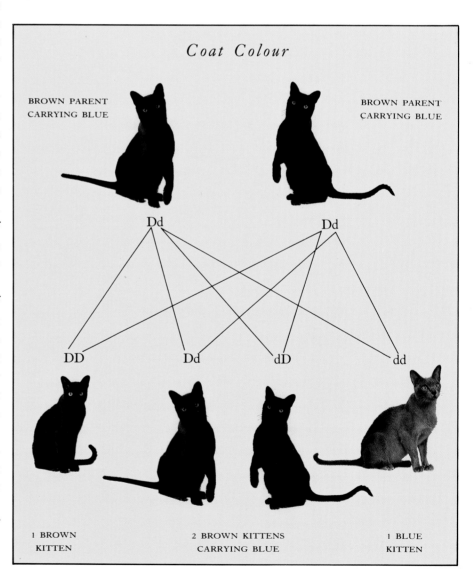

Coat Colour

BROWN PARENT CARRYING BLUE

BROWN PARENT CARRYING BLUE

Dd Dd

DD Dd dD dd

1 BROWN KITTEN

2 BROWN KITTENS CARRYING BLUE

1 BLUE KITTEN

Coat Length and Colour

SHORTHAIRED
BLACK

LONGHAIRED
BLUE

ALL SHORTHAIR BLACK
(CARRYING LONGHAIR)

| 9 SHORT-HAIRED BLACK | 3 LONG-HAIRED BLACK | 3 SHORT-HAIRED BLUE | 1 LONG-HAIRED BLUE |

Burmilla Programme

CHINCHILLA   LILAC BURMESE

*The two breeds selected for the first Burmilla programme mating (**ABOVE**); the first generation Burmilla (**RIGHT**); and (**BELOW**) examples of the variety of coat colour, length and pattern seen in subsequent generations.*

BURMILLA

ASIAN TICKED TABBY

BURMILLA

ASIAN TABBY

ASIAN SMOKE

BOMBAY   CREAM TIFFANIE

Coat Length and Colour

If you now consider two characters, those of coat length and colour, the possibilities increase. If a shorthaired black cat is mated with a longhaired blue, black coat colour is dominant to blue, and shorthair dominant to longhair. The progeny of the first cross will all be the same. If two of this first cross are mated together there is a possibility to produce four quite different phenotypes, different in both colour and fur length.

The diagram (*above*) shows a ratio of three blacks (dominant) to one blue (recessive) and three shorthairs (dominant) to one longhair (recessive).

Coat Pattern, Length and Colour

Involving a third character, coat pattern, can give rise to even more possibilities.

A recent programme to develop a new breed, the Burmilla – one of the Asian group of cats – shows these three genes, and how they are passed down. The original mating was a Chinchilla male (a longhaired variety with a black-tipped coat) to a Lilac Burmese (a shorthaired, dilute-recessive of unpatterned coat). As the patterned (Chinchilla) gene is dominant to the plain (Burmese) coat, and the gene for shorthair (Burmese) is dominant over longhair (Chinchilla), all the resultant kittens from this first outcross were shorthaired tipped of Burmese type, carrying the recessive longhair gene.

In theory, if two of these Burmillas were mated together, there are sixteen different colour combinations of coat length and pattern that could result; that is, eight colours with short coats and a corresponding eight with long coats. This comes back to Mendel's idea of ratios between dominant and recessive, and shows how two cats with the same coat colour, length and pattern can produce offspring that look completely different. It also demonstrates how complicated cat genetics become when more than one character has to be considered.

In practice, as breeders wanted to keep the Burmese type, first generation Burmillas were mated back to Burmese, and not to another Burmilla; which explains the relative rarity of the longhaired variety, the Tiffanie, in the early stages of the breeding programme.

This is only an outline for the principles of 'working' cat genetics and how new breeds can be created. In practice it includes much paperwork, research and mathematical calculation.

LONGHAIRED CATS OF PERSIAN TYPE

Longhaired Persian cats are one of the oldest known breeds of pedigree cat. The long, luxuriant coat gives them a glamorous look and instant appeal. Over the years, the type of the Persian has changed quite radically; today they are a short-faced, compact breed, with a long thick coat available in a myriad of colours.

History

Longhaired cats have been in Europe since the sixteenth century but are known to have existed in certain parts of the world long before then.

The original longhairs were found in Turkey in the region of Ankara and became known as Angoras; these should not be confused with the breed that we know today as the Angora (see 'Oriental Shorthairs'). Other longhaired cats were discovered in Persia, modern-day Iran, and because these had more profuse coats, they became more popular.

These early Persians, as they became known, looked quite different from those that we see on the modern show bench. Their faces were much longer and their

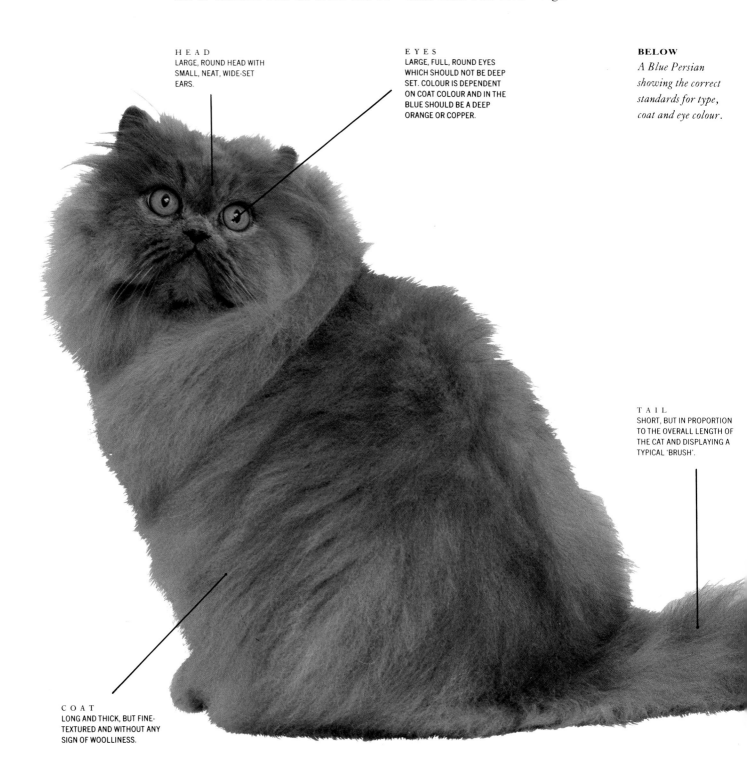

HEAD
LARGE, ROUND HEAD WITH SMALL, NEAT, WIDE-SET EARS.

EYES
LARGE, FULL, ROUND EYES WHICH SHOULD NOT BE DEEP SET. COLOUR IS DEPENDENT ON COAT COLOUR AND IN THE BLUE SHOULD BE A DEEP ORANGE OR COPPER.

BELOW
A Blue Persian showing the correct standards for type, coat and eye colour.

TAIL
SHORT, BUT IN PROPORTION TO THE OVERALL LENGTH OF THE CAT AND DISPLAYING A TYPICAL 'BRUSH'.

COAT
LONG AND THICK, BUT FINE-TEXTURED AND WITHOUT ANY SIGN OF WOOLLINESS.

coats neither as thick nor as luxuriant as their modern equivalents. The earliest record of a longhaired cat was of a brown tabby in the mid-nineteenth century and a solid black about the same time. By the turn of the century, more than twelve different colours were recognized, including what must be one of the most beautiful of all longhairs, the Chinchilla. Today there are more than sixty varieties and colour variations of the Persian.

Character and Temperament

Generally, Persian cats have quiet, gentle dispositions. The time they need for extra grooming is balanced by the fact that they do not demand constant personal attention. On the whole they are not a vociferous breed and will not pine if left alone when you are out at work during the day, although it is always kinder to have two cats rather than one, even if you do opt for Persians.

Type and Standard of Points

Persian cats all conform to the same general standard of points. Only the colour and pattern of their fur differs.

Persians are probably the most glamorous of all pedigree varieties. With long, luxuriant coats, brush-like tails, and a distinctive ruff around the neck, they look quite beautiful but need a lot of grooming to keep their coats in pristine condition. This takes time and any would-be owner of a Persian cat must be prepared to devote at least fifteen minutes a day to grooming their cat.

The standards require a small, elegant, but stocky cat showing large expressive eyes, a tiny nose and small, wide-set ears. The eye colour varies according to the coat colour but should always be complementary. Each colour variation calls for a slight modification in the standards but in general should still give the appearance of a typical Persian cat.

Coat Colours

SELF COLOURS

Black

The Black Persian is one of the oldest varieties and is still one of the most popular. As an adult, the fur should be jet black and the eyes deep copper – a striking combination. Although kittens may show faint ghost markings, or even a few white hairs, these are considered severe faults in an adult. Remember that for any black cat, longhaired or short-haired the full coat colour will take time to develop and so slight variations are acceptable up to about six months of age.

Blue

It is said that the Blue Persian was Queen Victoria's favourite breed of cat. Certainly it is one of the earliest Persian colours and is often thought to be the original colour of the breed (for this reason it is still one of the most popular variations). The coat should be a pale, even blue-grey with no shading or markings, and the eyes should be deep copper or orange.

ABOVE
Historically, black cats have had their ups and downs in the popularity stakes. This Black Persian well illustrates the beauty of the breed, groomed to perfection.

Chocolate

This is one of the newer colours and is a byproduct of the Colourpoint breeding programme, as is the lilac variation. The coat should be an even, solid, medium chocolate-brown, and the eyes a deep copper colour.

Cream

Cream Persians have been known since the end of the nineteenth century, when they were not particularly popular because they were considered to be rather bad, pale examples of a Red.

Today, the reverse is true and they are now admired for their beautiful colouring. It is considered a fault for the cream colour to be too hot; it should be an even pale cream, and the eyes deep copper.

Lilac

This is another variety of Persian from the Colourpoint breeding programme. The coat should be a solid pinkish dove-grey without any sign of masking or lighter or darker patches. The eye colour should be copper.

LEFT
This Chocolate Persian shows the correct warm, medium chocolate-brown colour required.

BELOW
Persian kittens appear so cute and appealing – but do you have the time to spend on their all-important grooming needs?

RIGHT

The Cream Persian is one of the best known of the solid colours of this breed, and is still very popular.

ABOVE

The Lilac Persian, like the Chocolate, is one of the newer colour varieties and has arisen by way of the Colourpoint breeding programme.

Red

This may well be one of the older colours of Persian cat but it is one of the most difficult to breed successfully – a common problem when breeding any red- or cream-coloured cat is to produce a coat without any tabby markings. For perfection the coat should be a clear, rich orange colour, solid to the roots. The eyes should be deep copper.

ABOVE AND LEFT
The glamorous look of the Persian belies the fact that it is a sturdy and robust breed that will enjoy outdoor access if this can be safely afforded. An added bonus, Persians will develop a fuller coat if allowed outdoors in the cooler months but, as a minus, will need more grooming!

LEFT
Glamorous White Persians are still one of the most popular of the Persian varieties.

White

The White was the original Angora colour but, as the Persian breed type has been preferred since the beginning of the twentieth century, these white cats no longer bear any resemblance to their Turkish ancestors. They now conform to the typical Persian breed standard, except that they can be found with three different colours of eyes: orange, blue and odd (one blue and one orange). The only extra consideration for White Persians is that their coats may need frequent bathing, especially if they are allowed some freedom outside the house.

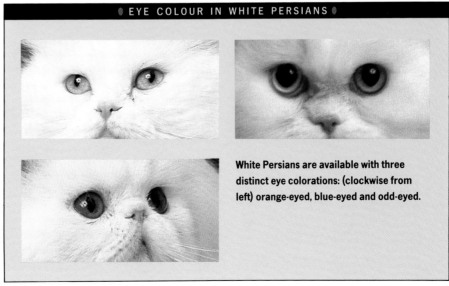

● EYE COLOUR IN WHITE PERSIANS ●

White Persians are available with three distinct eye colorations: (clockwise from left) orange-eyed, blue-eyed and odd-eyed.

RIGHT
*A Blue-Cream
Persian should show a
well-mingled mixture
of pastel tones of blue
and cream.*

*Cameo Persians have
a contrasting coat; the
undercoat should be as
pale as possible with
the tips shading to the
designated colour, such
as Red (**RIGHT**) or
Tortie (**FAR
RIGHT**).*

PATTERNED COLOURS

Bi-colour

These are two-tone cats which may be of
any colour mixed with white. Whatever
the main colour the eyes should be a deep
copper gold. As with any cat that has
white fur, Bi-colours may need to be
bathed occasionally to keep their coats
sparkling.

Blue-Cream

This is a form of the Tortie and so is
usually a female-only variety. As with all
Torties, any males produced are almost
invariably sterile. The Blue-Cream was
developed by mating a Blue and a Cream
together. The standards of the UK require that the two colours are well-
mingled without any obvious patches of a
solid colour. In the USA the reverse is
true and clearly separated areas of definite
colour are required. In either case, the
eyes should be deep copper or orange.

Cameo

These are Persian cats with a restricted tipped coat, related to the Chinchilla and Smoke. There are three densities of Cameo, shell, shaded and smoke, depending on how much tipping appears on each strand of fur. Shell Cameos have just the smallest amount of colour at the end of each hair; shaded have pigmentation further down the hair shaft, and smokes only reveal white undercoat when the fur is moved or when the cat is walking. For each of these three varieties there are three acceptable colours: red, cream and tortie.

BELOW
Cream-and-White Bi-colour showing the required distinct patches of colour.

RIGHT
The Chinchilla is one of the most popular of Persian breeds, and no wonder; it has an almost ethereal look, as each strand of white fur is tipped in black, giving a 'sparkling' effect. Note the required green eyes, outlined in black and the brick-red nose, again, outlined in black.

Chinchilla

In the USA the Chinchilla conforms exactly to the standards laid down for the Persian breed in general; in the UK the cat is allowed to be more finely boned, with a tendency to a longer muzzle than seen in most Persians.

The Chinchilla is one of the most popular of all longhaired breeds and not without reason. Its white coat, lightly tipped at the edges with black, give the cat a sparkling, almost ethereal and fairy-like appearance.

The coat should be evenly tipped with black on the head, back, legs, tail and flanks; the underpart should be pure white. The nose should be a distinctive brick-red outlined in black. The large expressive eyes should be green, without any trace of blue, with eyelids outlined in black giving an effect of applied mascara.

Colourpoint
(USA, HIMALAYAN)

This is a genetically engineered breed, the result of crossing a Blue Persian with a Siamese; this introduced the restricted coat pattern or Himalayan factor. Whatever colour the points, the type should be as for a Persian, but with the colour restricted to the face, ears, tail and legs. However, the eye colour differs to the Persian type in that a deep blue is the required standard for all Colourpoints, similar to that of the Siamese.

Colourpoints are available in just as many colours as are Siamese: seal, blue, chocolate, lilac, red, cream, tortie, tabby and tortie-tabby (torbie). These colours, and the associated colour of nose leather and paw pads, should be identical to those laid down for Siamese (*see 'Siamese' for more details*).

*Colourpoint (USA, Himalayan) Persians show the restricted 'Himalayan' coat pattern that was introduced by mating a Persian to a Siamese, and they are available in just as many colours and patterns as the Siamese. Whatever the colour, it is important for the points to be restricted to ears, face, legs and tail only. The examples shown here are Tortie-Tabby (**RIGHT**), Seal (**BELOW LEFT**), Blue (**BOTTOM**) and Cream (**BELOW RIGHT**).*

ABOVE
The Golden Persian
(**LEFT**) *and Shaded*
Golden (**RIGHT**) *are*
related to the
Chinchilla and show
what happens when
the sex-linked red gene
is introduced to the
Chinchilla breed; they
were originally known
as 'Golden
Chinchillas'.

Golden

In recent years the Chinchilla has shown that it hides a recessive gene, the red factor. This has given rise to the Golden Persian. The coat should show the same amount of tipping as seen in the Chinchilla, but the base colour must be a rich cream tipped with brown, shading to a lighter hue on the underparts. Just as a Shaded Silver can be produced from the Chinchilla, so can a Shaded Golden; this shows much denser tipping. Both varieties of golden should have vivid green eyes like the Chinchilla.

Pewter

The Pewter is the result of mating a Chinchilla with any one of the self-coloured Persians. Like the Chinchilla, it has a tipped coat but the density of the tipping is much heavier. Deep copper is the required eye colour.

Shaded Silver

This is a more heavily tipped type of Chinchilla, and in many fancies it is not recognized as a separate breed. In general it has similar markings to the Chinchilla, including the brick-red nose and eyes outlined in black; it is only the density of the tipping that distinguishes it.

ABOVE
The Pewter is almost a
'halfway house'
between the Chinchilla
and Smoke, being
neither as pale as the
Chinchilla nor as dark
as the Smoke.

RIGHT
Shaded Silvers are a close relation of the Chinchilla, showing the same eye and nose colours, but feature a more densely tipped coat.

RIGHT
Tabby cats reflect the wild-cat coat pattern that would be needed for camouflage in the wild, but are now bred in many different colours. The Silver Tabby is one of the most popular colours.

BELOW
Persian Smokes can be seen in many colours, but the Black Smoke is the classic. Whatever the colour, the undercoat should be as white as possible with the definite colour most apparent on the back, head and feet. The eye colour should always be copper or orange.

LEFT
This Red-Tabby Persian shows a really full, long and luxuriant coat so typical of this group in general.

Smoke

This is another variety of Persian that has
been seen since the nineteenth century. It
was originally bred by crossing a Chinchilla with a Black Persian. The tipping
on a Smoke is almost the reverse of that
on a Chinchilla; it is only the very base of
the coat that shows the pale hue, with the
tipped effect taking up most of the length
of the fur. Over the years Smokes have
been produced in a variety of colours and
today ten of these are recognized. Whatever the coat colour the eyes should be
copper or orange.

Tabby

Brown Tabbies are possibly the oldest
variety of Persian, but as with most
things time moves on and even this classic
pattern is now available in ten colours:
brown, silver, blue, chocolate, lilac, red,
and four colours of tortie-tabby (torbie).
Because the Tabby conforms to the general standards of Persian, particularly in
the profuse coat, it is often difficult to
distinguish the tabby markings. Most
Tabbies should show deep copper eyes;
however, in the silver this colour should
be green or hazel.

ABOVE
Brown-and-White Tabbies should show solid black markings set off against a rich brown background and the white area should be well defined.

Tabby-and-White

Tabby-and-Whites are accepted in the same colours as Tabbies. They should display even, solid areas of white on their coats and the eye colour should be the same as specified for Tabbies.

Tortoiseshell

Torties are generally recognized as being a female-only variety. The tortoiseshell colour is classically a patched selection of red, cream and black. However, it is possible to have Torties in the recessive and dilute colours of blue, chocolate and lilac. Whatever the colour of coat, the eyes should be deep copper or orange.

Tortie-and-White
(*USA, CALICO*)

The colour variations are the same as for Tortoiseshell, as is the eye colour. The only difference is that the coat should show solid white patches intermingled with the tortie markings.

ABOVE
Blue-and-White Tabbies should have blue markings against a beige background.

LEFT
Tortoiseshell cats are most usually a female-only variety as their coat pattern is inherited from a sex-linked gene. A Brown-Tortie Persian should show a coat that has colours of black, red and cream.

BELOW
Exotic Shorthairs are truly cats of Persian type, quite distinct from the British Shorthairs, but with short fur! They are available in all the colours and patterns accepted for the Persians.

ABOVE
Tortie-and-White cats (Calico in the USA) must have at least one-third white in their coat, and the colours accepted are the same as for the tortie colours in general.

EXOTIC SHORTHAIR

I t may seem strange to include a short-haired variety of cat in a longhaired category. It is an anomaly, but the Exotic is truly a shorthaired Persian; it conforms to all requirements of the Persian breed, displays the same temperament, is available in all the recognized colours for Persians, the only difference being that it has a short coat.

◗ ADVANTAGES ◗

◗ Sweet-natured and affectionate.
◗ Not too demanding.
◗ Good with children.
◗ Not vociferous; females are quieter than most breeds when on call.
◗ Within reason, cope with being left alone at home.

◗ DISADVANTAGES ◗

◗ Require thorough daily grooming.
◗ Shed fur on carpets and furnishings.

LONGHAIRED CATS OF NON-PERSIAN TYPE

These breeds are all completely different, come from various parts of the world, and many are quite recently developed 'designer' breeds; the only common factor is that their fur is long, but usually neither as long nor as profuse as in the full Persian breeds. Each breed displays its own personality, needs and demands and so must be treated as a separate entity.

ANGORA
(*see Oriental Shorthairs*)

BALINESE
(*see Siamese*)

BIRMAN

History

These are often thought of as the sacred temple cats of Burma, and they originate from this country. They are an enchanting breed and the distinctive coat pattern, with white paws, has given rise to a delightful legend. It is said that a cat, sensing that the high priest was dying, walked over to him and gently put its paws on the priest's frail body to offer companionship during his last hours; as the priest died, the cat's paws were turned purest white and that is how they have stayed to this day. Because of the cat's devotion to the priest, it is further told that each time a Birman cat dies, the soul of a priest accompanies it to heaven.

These tales are charming, but in actuality the breed was probably developed much more recently by crossing a Siamese with a Bi-colour Longhair; this definitely occurred in France in the early 1920s. The first Birmans were of a similar coat colour to the Seal-point Siamese, a pale milky cream with deep seal points and, of course, the distinctive white paws.

Character and Temperament

The Birman is a clever breed, but not as demanding or noisy as the Siamese or Burmese. Their semi-long coats do need extra grooming, but not as much as the Persian Longhairs require. They make ideal pets, and are good with children and other animals.

Type and Standard of Points

The Birman should be a medium-sized cat, with a long, silky coat – although it should never be as long or as dense as the Persian's.

Over the years, Birmans have been bred in many different colours, and can now be seen in twenty variations. The original Seal is possibly the most popular, but the Birman is available in blue, chocolate, lilac, red, cream, and the associated tortie and tabby patterns. Whatever the colour, the coat should be evenly marked with points confined to the face, ears, tail and legs, but with the paws white. These markings must be symmetrical, with the 'gloves' on the front legs ending in a straight line and extending no further than the top of the paws; the rear leg markings, 'gauntlets', should stretch up to the back of the hock. In all Birmans, the eye colour should be bright sapphire blue.

BELOW

Birmans originate from Burma although, unlike Burmese which also come from the same country, they are a longhaired variety. These are Blue-point Birmans.

RIGHT

This Seal-point was the first ever Birman to be made up to the Grand title in the UK. This beautiful neuter boy really displays the finer points required for this breed.

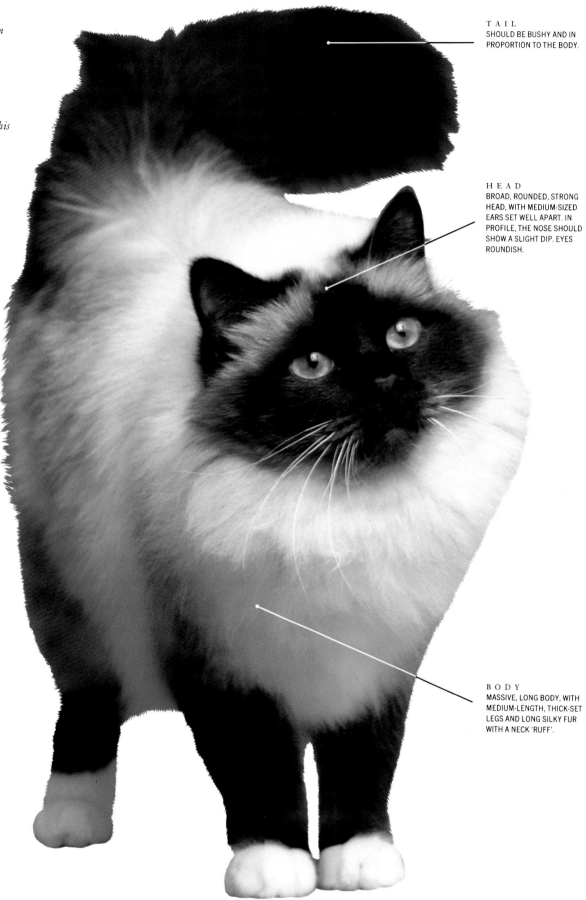

TAIL
SHOULD BE BUSHY AND IN PROPORTION TO THE BODY.

HEAD
BROAD, ROUNDED, STRONG HEAD, WITH MEDIUM-SIZED EARS SET WELL APART. IN PROFILE, THE NOSE SHOULD SHOW A SLIGHT DIP. EYES ROUNDISH.

BODY
MASSIVE, LONG BODY, WITH MEDIUM-LENGTH, THICK-SET LEGS AND LONG SILKY FUR WITH A NECK 'RUFF'.

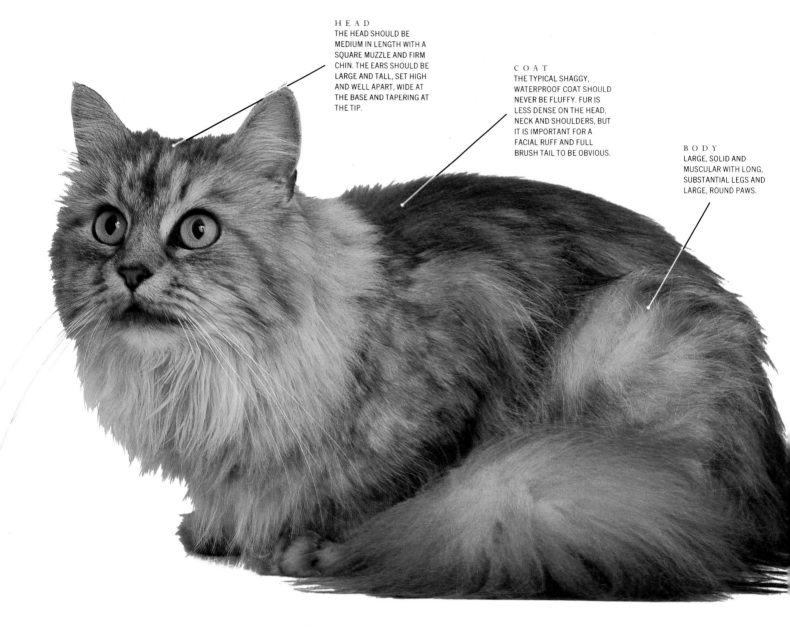

HEAD
THE HEAD SHOULD BE MEDIUM IN LENGTH WITH A SQUARE MUZZLE AND FIRM CHIN. THE EARS SHOULD BE LARGE AND TALL, SET HIGH AND WELL APART, WIDE AT THE BASE AND TAPERING AT THE TIP.

COAT
THE TYPICAL SHAGGY, WATERPROOF COAT SHOULD NEVER BE FLUFFY. FUR IS LESS DENSE ON THE HEAD, NECK AND SHOULDERS, BUT IT IS IMPORTANT FOR A FACIAL RUFF AND FULL BRUSH TAIL TO BE OBVIOUS.

BODY
LARGE, SOLID AND MUSCULAR WITH LONG, SUBSTANTIAL LEGS AND LARGE, ROUND PAWS.

ABOVE
This Silver-Tabby Maine Coon displays the typical standards of the breed.

CYMRIC
(see Manx, British Shorthairs)

MAINE COON

History

As the name suggests, this was origi-nally an American breed although, in recent years, they have been imported into the UK where they are now becom-ing increasingly popular. The name com-es in part from the state of Maine, where they were first seen, with 'Coon' being derived from the brush-like tail that is reminiscent of a racoon, and so typical of this breed. An alternative, and more romantic, notion is that Marie Antoinette sent her beloved cats to America to escape the French Revolution and these were the ancestors of the modern breed.

The Maine Coon was recognized in some American cat fancies as early as 1967, but it was not until the 1980s that they became popular in the UK, where they are now accepted.

Character and Temperament

Although Maine Coons can grow to be large cats, they have very sweet natures. They are playful and friendly, and make delightful pets.

Type and Standard of Points

The Maine Coon is a large, sturdy, extremely handsome semi-longhaired cat. The head should be long, but not as long as the Siamese, with a definite squared-off muzzle. The legs are long. The coat is heavy and tends to be more prolific around the neck (giving the typical ruff effect), the belly, legs and tail. The coat is not as profuse as on the Persian Longhairs, and does not require as much grooming; however, it is a thick, dense coat that provides the cat with insulation during the cold winter months in New England. The classic Maine Coon is a tabby-and-white, but the breed is acceptable in almost any coat colour and pattern, and the eye colour may be green, hazel, copper, blue, or odd-eyed.

RIGHT
Brown Tortie-Tabby Maine Coons should show black and red markings against a background of warm copper.

LEFT
Tortie-and-White Maine Coons should have a coat predominantly made up of the base colour, with white fur ideally on the face, chest, legs and feet.

RIGHT

*Norwegian Forest
Cats are a new and
interesting breed; they
have the unique ability
to climb up sheer rock
faces, and are both
elegant and energetic.
This Blue Tabby-and-
White typifies the type
required for
this breed.*

NORWEGIAN FOREST CAT

History

T his breed is a little similar to the
Maine Coon, but developed in the
cold climate of northern Scandinavia.
The thick coat provided the cat with
warmth in severe weather. In Norse
tales, legends make reference to a fairy
cat, and this may well have been the
Norwegian Forest Cat as its plume-like
tail has an ethereal look. It is an excellent
climber, able to get to areas most cats
could not reach, and this has added to the
mystique of the breed. It has been seen at
shows in Norway since before World
War II, but was not recognized by the
Fédération Internationale Féline (FIFe)
until 1977. The breed is popular in the
USA, but has only recently been imported to the UK.

Character and Temperament

The Norwegian Forest Cat is a lively and
independent cat. It is a good hunter and,
with its thick, waterproof coat, enjoys
being allowed freedom in a garden. It
does like human company and prefers
not to be left alone for any great length
of time.

Type and Standard of Points

The head should be roughly triangular in
shape, with high-set large ears. The nose
should be straight and the eyes an almond
shape. The thick, waterproof coat should
be long, with long guard hairs covering
the dense undercoat.

LEFT

*Norwegian Forest
Cats come in a variety
of colours and
patterns; this is a
Brown Tabby-and-
White.*

BODY
THIS IS A BIG STRONG BREED
OF CAT, WITH A LONG BODY
AND LEGS; THE BACK LEGS
SHOULD BE HIGHER THAN
THE FORELEGS. THE COAT IS
SEMI-LONG, WITH A GLOSSY,
WATERPROOF OVERCOAT,
AND SHOULD DISPLAY A
'RUFF' AROUND THE NECK.

HEAD
THE HEAD SHOULD BE
TRIANGULAR IN SHAPE, AND
IN PROFILE BE STRAIGHT
WITH A STRONG CHIN. EARS
ARE SET HIGH, WITH GOOD
WIDTH AT THE BASE OF THE
EAR. THE TIPS SHOULD BE
TUFTED WITH LONG HAIR
SEEN OUT OF THE EARS. EYES
ARE LARGE AND SET AT AN
OBLIQUE.

TAIL
BUSHY TAIL, LONG ENOUGH
THAT IT REACHES THE NECK.

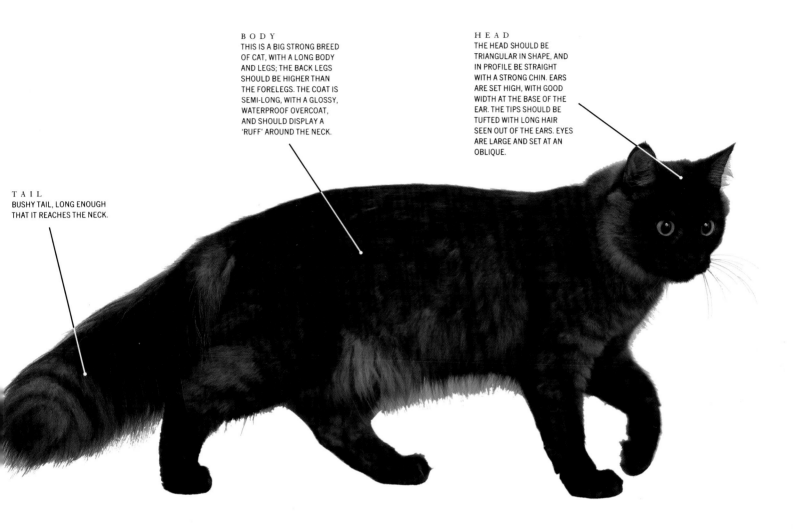

ABOVE
*This Smoke
Norwegian Forest Cat
really shows the
required 'brush' tail to
perfection.*

RIGHT
*Peke-faced Persians do
not conform to the
general standards laid
down for the Persian
breed. They are
neither accepted nor
bred in the UK, but
are available in the
USA in as many
colours and patterns as
acceptable for the
Persians.*

PEKE-FACED

T~ his is a somewhat controversial breed
that is essentially an ultra-type Persian. The breed has been put in this
section, as some of the traits it displays
are not desirable in the usual Persian type
of longhair. The nose is so short as to be
almost flat on the face. There is also a
very strong indentation between the eyes,
giving rise to a typically furrowed brow
and causing the eyes to be large and
protruding. This is a breed only seen in
America, although some ultra-type Persians are bred in the UK, but not to such
an extreme. In temperament and character, they are very similar to the Persian
Longhairs and, in the fancies where they
are regarded as a separate breed, are
available in all the colours recognized for
Persians.

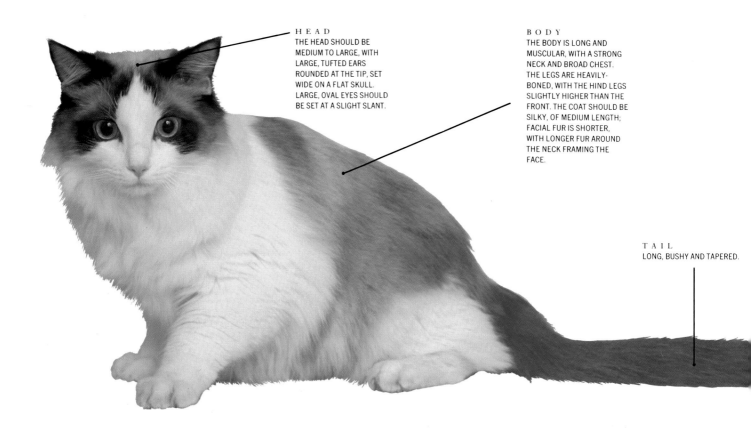

HEAD
THE HEAD SHOULD BE MEDIUM TO LARGE, WITH LARGE, TUFTED EARS ROUNDED AT THE TIP, SET WIDE ON A FLAT SKULL. LARGE, OVAL EYES SHOULD BE SET AT A SLIGHT SLANT.

BODY
THE BODY IS LONG AND MUSCULAR, WITH A STRONG NECK AND BROAD CHEST. THE LEGS ARE HEAVILY-BONED, WITH THE HIND LEGS SLIGHTLY HIGHER THAN THE FRONT. THE COAT SHOULD BE SILKY, OF MEDIUM LENGTH; FACIAL FUR IS SHORTER, WITH LONGER FUR AROUND THE NECK FRAMING THE FACE.

TAIL
LONG, BUSHY AND TAPERED.

ABOVE
Bi-colour Ragdoll, showing the correct 'V' marking on the forehead.

RAGDOLL

History

Much controversy surrounds the history of this breed, which gained recognition in the USA in the 1960s. The charm of the Ragdoll is said to lie in the fact that it will flop in your arms when handled, but this is not uncommon in any cat that trusts its owner.

The first Ragdoll kittens are said to have been born in California to a white Persian queen who had mismated and, after suffering a broken pelvis in a car accident, gave birth to a litter of kittens that flopped when handled. This would be genetically impossible, as the result of a road accident cannot cause the cat's genetic make-up to be changed and so be passed ·on to future generations. The truth of the Ragdoll's background is open to speculation. Looking at the varieties of Ragdoll accepted today, it is likely that the breed has an ancestry linked with Siamese, Colourpoints or Birmans.

Character and Temperament

The Ragdoll is possibly one of the most laid-back of all breeds of domesticated cats. It is relatively undemanding, very tolerant of most situations, and is gentle and relaxed. It is said that these cats have a lower pain threshold than most, but it is a debatable point, and certainly not one that should be tested.

Type and Standard of Points

There are three basic patterns of Ragdoll that are accepted: bi-colour, colourpoint and mitted, and the colour for each may be seal, blue, chocolate or lilac. The coloured areas are generally restricted to the face, legs and tail, in a manner similar to the Colourpoints' and Birmans' restrictive markings. The fur is particularly long on the chest and abdomen, on the back of the head (giving a distinct ruff), and on the tail, which should be thick and full. The eyes should always be blue.

SOMALI
(see Abyssinian, Other Shorthairs)

TIFFANIE
(see Asian Cats, Other Shorthairs)

TURKISH VAN

History

This is a natural breed of cat which was first discovered around the shores of Lake Van, a remote area of Turkey. The most astonishing fact about the breed is that it not only likes water, but really enjoys going for a swim. It is probably descended from the Angora, one of the original varieties of longhaired cat, and is distinguished by attractive auburn markings around the face and on the tail. Turkish Vans have a distinct white 'thumb print' mark between their ears which the Turkish people call the mark of Allah and so, in their native homeland, these cats are treated with great respect. A trip to modern-day Istanbul will reveal street cats that, although mostly shorthaired, are generally white with auburn markings. In the early 1950s the first pair was brought back to Britain and a breeding programme started; by 1969 they were granted official recognition. Today they grace the show benches on both sides of the Atlantic.

Character and Temperament

Turkish Vans are very friendly, sociable and intelligent, and they like company. They have soft voices, and are happy to live quietly inside your home, as long as they are given attention and the odd game to play. They like to be offered the opportunity for a swim and so, if you do not have a pool, let the cat take some exercise in the bath.

Type and Standard of Points

The classic form of Turkish Van is a chalk-white semi-longhair cat with auburn markings restricted to the head, ears and tail, and with amber eyes. Over the years, various other colours have been noted and the Van is now accepted in both auburn and cream colours, and with amber, blue or odd-coloured eyes. The head is a short wedge shape, with a longish nose, and the ears are large and pointed.

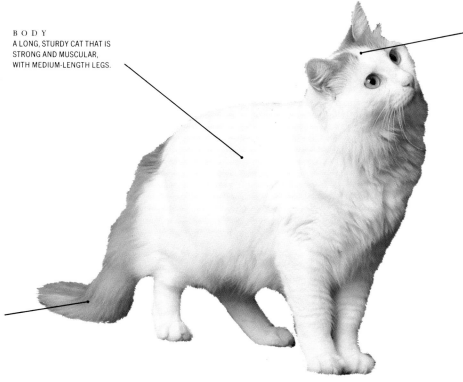

BODY
A LONG, STURDY CAT THAT IS STRONG AND MUSCULAR, WITH MEDIUM-LENGTH LEGS.

RIGHT
The Classic Turkish Van has a white coat, with auburn markings and amber eyes.

HEAD
HEAD SHOULD BE A SHORT WEDGE AND SHOW A LONG NOSE; IN PROFILE, NOSE SHOULD BE STRAIGHT BUT WITH A SLIGHTLY NOTICEABLE DIP. EARS ARE LARGE, SET HIGH ON HEAD AND FAIRLY CLOSE TOGETHER. THE EYES SHOULD BE LARGE AND OVAL.

TAIL
THE TAIL SHOULD BE BRUSH-LIKE AND IN BALANCE WITH THE OVERALL LENGTH OF THE CAT.

BRITISH AND AMERICAN SHORTHAIRS

British and American Shorthairs gain their names from the fact that they are the indigenous breeds of these two countries. Although American Shorthairs probably originated in Great Britain, travelling to America around the time of the Pilgrim Fathers in the early seventeenth century, the two breeds are still very similar with only minor differences required in their standards.

◦ HISTORY ◦

The history of this breed goes back to Roman times and it is thought that the invading Roman troops first brought shorthaired cats to Britain. Written records for the British Shorthair only go back to the turn of the century although it is clear, from old paintings and engravings, that they had been around for several hundred years before this.

Shorthairs were probably originally kept for their mousing ability and for the fact that, unlike the Persians and Angoras also seen at this time, they did not need human help with their grooming. They were a self-sufficient variety, which provided a useful service to man, and it is recorded that most ships setting sail for the New World included several cats on the cargo list.

The oldest recorded type of shorthaired cat was the tabby. Elegantly and attractively marked with darker stripes or spots, the tabby's coat reflects the coat pattern of its wild cat ancestry; the cats worshipped in Ancient Egypt were similar tabbies, although their coats tended to be ticked. On the show bench today, Tabbies are still very popular but the newer, glamorous Silver Tabby is more in evidence than the original Brown Tabby, which seems to have been ignored in the breeding programmes of recent years.

The self-coloured varieties of British and American Shorthairs are among the most popular, the most obvious example being the Blue. They are also available in various other colours and patterns; more recent introductions include the Tipped, showing the coat markings associated with the Chinchilla, and the Colourpoint, a true British cat but with the distinctive restricted coat pattern usually associated with the Siamese.

BELOW
The British Shorthair is essentially a chunky feline, well-illustrated by this orange-eyed White.

Character and Temperament

British and American Shorthairs can grow to be some of the largest domestic cats, but their gentle and shy dispositions have caused them to be described as the 'gentle giants'. They are loving and affectionate, have quiet voices and, rather like the Persians, do not continuously demand their owners' attentions. Generally, they do not seem to have the wanderlust of the foreign breeds and will not mind being confined to an apartment. Even if given the freedom of a garden, they are unlikely to wander far.

Type and Standard of Points

British and American Shorthairs should be large, strong, sturdy and muscular. The male is larger than the female, and more obviously so than in most other breeds. Neuters, especially the males, do have a tendency to obesity, so a close watch should be kept on their diet.

Typically the chest should be deep and broad with short, strong legs and neat, rounded paws. The head should be wide and rounded and in males should show definite jowls. In profile the nose should show a 'stop', and the jaw should show a level bite without any sign of being either overshot or undershot. The ears should be small and set wide apart. In all colours and patterns the coat should be short, crisp and dense but without appearing woolly; the only exception to this is in the Manx varieties.

The overall look for the British is for a chunky, cobby cat without the extreme facial expression of the Persian; it is usually accepted for the American Shorthair to be slightly heavier and in general longer than its British counterpart. The colours available are almost the same as those acceptable for the Persian, with more colours for the American Shorthair than the British.

Coat Colours

SELF-COLOURS

White

Although the coat colour should remain the same – an even, pure white – three different eye colours are acceptable: orange, blue and odd-eyed. In a young kitten, the odd patch of darker colour on the top of the head is permissible; by adulthood any such markings should have disappeared and if they remain, are considered a serious fault.

Black

A glossy, jet black is the required coat colour. Moreover, the colour should be solid to the roots, with no trace of rustiness, tabby markings, white hairs or patches. The eyes should be a deep copper without any trace of green.

BELOW
The British Black is typical of this breed; although the kittens are most appealing, remember that they will grow into very large cats when adult, especially if male!

Blue

This is probably the best known of all the Shorthair varieties; in Europe, it is known as the Chartreux. The coat should be a distinctive blue-grey, without any silver ticking, and the colour solid to the roots. The eye colour should be deep copper, as in the Black.

Cream

An even, pale-coloured cream coat is desired; in practice this is hard to achieve and many cats do show faint 'ghost' tabby or spotted markings. The eye colour should be deep copper.

Chocolate

This should be an even, solid, medium chocolate-brown, and the eye colour should be copper.

RIGHT
The British Blue, showing the required golden-copper eye colour, can grow to be an exceedingly large cat.

ABOVE
British Chocolates are a relatively new colour and, like their Persian counterparts, have arrived by way of the Colourpoint breeding programme.

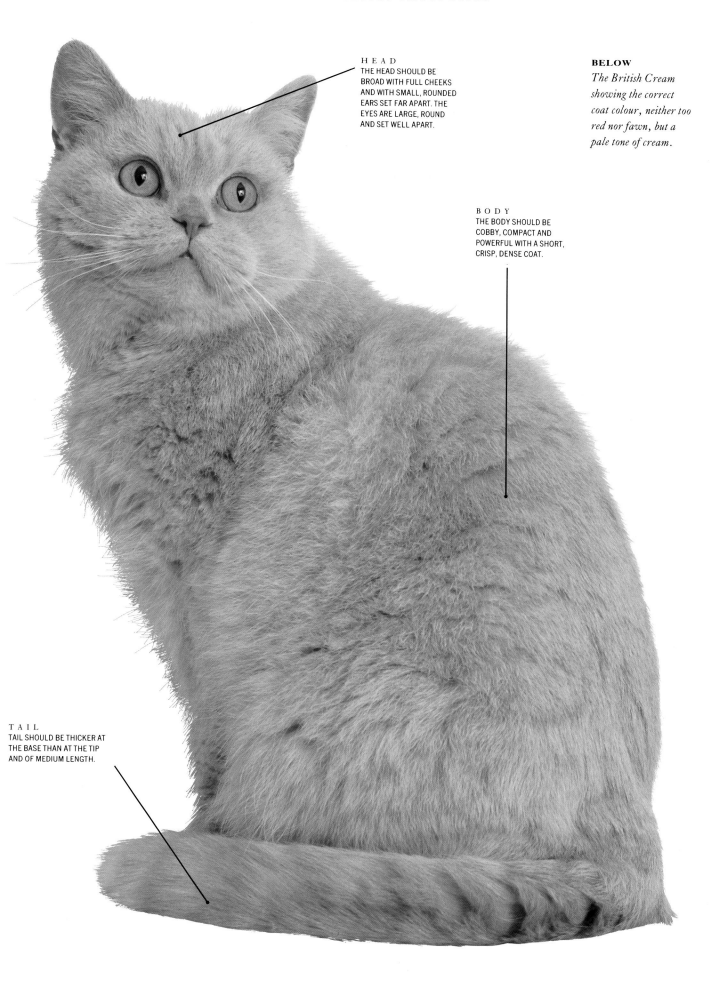

HEAD
THE HEAD SHOULD BE BROAD WITH FULL CHEEKS AND WITH SMALL, ROUNDED EARS SET FAR APART. THE EYES ARE LARGE, ROUND AND SET WELL APART.

BELOW
The British Cream showing the correct coat colour, neither too red nor fawn, but a pale tone of cream.

BODY
THE BODY SHOULD BE COBBY, COMPACT AND POWERFUL WITH A SHORT, CRISP, DENSE COAT.

TAIL
TAIL SHOULD BE THICKER AT THE BASE THAN AT THE TIP AND OF MEDIUM LENGTH.

Lilac

A solid pinkish dove-grey coat combines with a copper eye colour. The Lilac and Chocolate are quite recent colours, by-products of the Colourpoint breeding programme.

BELOW
Father and daughter of one of the newer colours, Lilac, showing how much larger the male may become in comparison to the female.

ABOVE
The American Shorthair varies slightly from the standards laid down for the British; in general, it is a longer cat and less heavily boned.

TABBIES

British Red Spotted Tabby

American Brown Tabby

British Silver Tabby

PATTERNED COLOURS

Tabby

These are seen in three patterns: classic, mackerel and spotted, and are most often brown, blue, red and silver. Whatever the colour, the markings should be a much deeper hue than the background; for example, Brown Tabbies should have a sable background colour with black markings, the Reds should have a rich red background with distinctively deeper red markings, and the Silver Tabbies a clear silver body colour with black markings. The eye colour depends on that of the coat; in Reds and Browns this should be copper or orange, and green or hazel in the Silvers.

BELOW
Spotted Tabbies are a very popular breed, the Silvers in particular. They should show numerous, well-defined spots throughout the coat.

Tortie

As in the Persian, a well-mingled mixture of colours is desired in the UK, without any solid patch of any one colour. The most popular and most commonly seen of this female-only variety is the Blue-Cream. They can, however, be seen in a variety of colours and the eye colour should be the same as that laid down for the main colour of the coat.

Tortie-and-White

These have been produced by mating a Tortie to a Bi-colour and are seen in the same number of colours as Torties. It is important for the white areas to be clearly defined, and the eye colour should be as for the Tortie.

Colourpoint

This is a more recent colour variation, genetically engineered by breeders. The original cross was between a British and a Longhair Colourpoint, which resulted in early generations showing slightly fluffy coats; this has now been eradicated and Colourpoints today have typical British coats and type. They are available in all the colours seen in Siamese and, unlike most British, have blue eyes.

ABOVE
*A good contrast between the basic coat colour and the points is required for the British Colourpoint, as depicted here in a young Blue Colourpoint (**LEFT**) and Tortie Colourpoint (**RIGHT**).*

LEFT
A Chocolate Colourpoint clearly showing the required coat colour pattern restriction.

ABOVE
The British Tipped is a British Shorthair with the Chinchilla gene introduced to produce the distinctive tipping to the coat.

● TIPPING ●

Tipped: the dark colour is restricted to the hair tips

Smoke: the dark colour extends almost to the roots

Tipped

This is a British cat hiding behind a shorthaired version of the Chinchilla's coat. The tips of the fur should be black with pure white underparts, the nose should be brick-red outlined in black, and the eyes should be outlined in black. The Tipped are now bred in a variety of colours, but whatever the colour, the pigmentation should be confined to the extreme tips of the fur only.

Smoke

Effectively the reverse of the British Tipped, the Smoke exhibits a silver undermantle with a denser colour taking up most of the length of the fur. The main colour can be any acceptable for the British Shorthair breed in general. Adults should not show vestiges of tabby markings or any white hair in the coat. Eyes are copper, gold or orange.

Bi-colour

This is a two-tone cat, which can be any of the recognized colours and patterns acceptable for the British, but it must display symmetrical patches of white with the background colour.

ABOVE LEFT
This may look like a black cat, but it is a British Smoke; the difference lies in the fact that the undercoat is silver, and not black to the roots.

ABOVE RIGHT
A British Blue Bi-colour; one of many of the colours available for this coat pattern.

RIGHT
The British Bi-colour should have patches of the self-colour and white, with the patches, for perfection, being as symmetrical as possible as seen in this Cream-and-White Bi-colour.

RIGHT
The classic Rumpy Manx has no vestige of a tail and, as seen in this Tortie-and-White, should have a rump that stands higher than the shoulders.

BELOW LEFT
A White Stumpy Manx, showing the distinctive rounded rump required for the breed standards.

BELOW RIGHT
An odd-eyed Tailed Manx, unacceptable for the show bench requirements, but useful to any Manx breeding programme.

MANX
(and Cymric)

The Manx is unlike most British Shorthairs and not just because it usually does not have a tail. The type required for a Manx is less extreme than that required for most British and Americans cats. Also, the Manx nose is usually a bit longer. The coat is accepted in any colour or combination of colours, is thicker and more prone to matting than the classic British Shorthair coat, and for this reason, needs extra grooming.

Manx are generally seen in four forms: Rumpy, Stumpy, Tailed and Cymric. Rumpies have no tail at all and, for perfection, a small dip should be noticeable at the base of the spine where the tail would have been; this is the only type of Manx recognized for showing purposes in the UK, although the other types may be used for breeding. Stumpies have a small amount of tail, more like a bump at the base of the spine, and it is possible to have tailed varieties of Manx too. All Manx cats should have back legs that are considerably longer than the front ones, which gives rise to their typical, rather unusual, rabbit-like gait.

The Cymric is a longhaired variety of Manx and is comparatively rare, especially in the UK. In character and temperament, Manx and Cymric are just like other British varieties and make the most delightful pets.

ABOVE
The Cymric, rare in Britain but popular in the United States, is a longhaired variety of Manx.

ORIENTAL
SHORTHAIRS

The Oriental is very much an artificially created type of breed. Although solid-coloured cats of Siamese type have been seen for many years, usually as the result of a mismating, they were not popular until the 1950s. Then, experimental matings took place between Siamese and Russian Blues, among others, and led the way to the development of the Havana. A byproduct of this breeding programme was the Oriental Lilac.

these are available in just as many colours. Genetically, this section could produce an almost unlimited variety of coat colours and patterns.

Character and Temperament

Oriental cats are basically Siamese cats without the restrictive, Himalayan, pattern in their coats. They have exactly the same type and conformation as the Siamese, and their temperament is the same too: outgoing personalities that demand a lot of attention.

Orientals have exceedingly loud voices and will often instigate the conversation – they are not like well brought-up children who only speak when they are spoken to. They want to be involved in every household activity, be it sharing your bed or helping you wash the dishes. Just like dogs, they love to play retrieving games and derive hours of pleasure from a simple piece of screwed-up paper. They do not like to be left for any length of time on their own, and would benefit from a feline companion if you are out at work all day.

Type and Standard of Points

Whatever the coat colour or pattern, the standard requires the shape and type of the cat to be exactly the same as that of the Siamese (*see 'Siamese'*). This means that the Oriental is a medium-sized cat that should feel firm and muscular. It is slender and elegant, but despite its shape and size should feel heavy. Orientals should never be overtly skinny or feel too light in weight.

The eye colour varies to complement the coat colour, and the eye shape should show the typical Oriental slant. The ears should be wide apart and, when viewed from the front, should give the appearance of a triangle from the tip of the two ears down to the point of the nose. In profile, the nose should be straight.

ABOVE
The Oriental Black, with the typical glossy solid black coat, typifies the elegance of the Oriental group of cats.

History

Solid colours, other than the original Lilac, soon became possible, and today we have Orientals recognized in ten colours and the associated seven colours of the Tortie.

As the popularity of the Orientals increased, and breeders became aware of the genetic possibilities of different coat patterns, a new programme was started. This gave rise, by mating back to Tabby-point Siamese, to Spotted, Classic and Mackerel Tabbies, in a variety of different colour variations. The Ticked Tabby arrived by crossing a Seal-point Siamese with an Abyssinian. It is equally possible to breed Orientals with a smoke coat, and

Coat Colours

SELF-COLOURS

These must be of the same colour overall, solid to the roots and without any sign of shading, barring, tabby markings or white hairs. These are some of the colours currently recognized:

Havana

This is a rich, warm brown with brown nose leather and pinky-brown paw pads. The eye colour should be vivid green.

White

A clear, bright white is the required colour, with pale-pink nose and paw pads, and brilliant sapphire-blue eyes.

Black

A solid jet black is required, with paw pads and nose leather the same, and vivid green eyes.

Blue

This should be a light to medium blue, with nose leather and paw pads the same, and the eyes green.

Lilac

A pinkish frosty-grey is required, with nose leather and paw pads lavender, and the eyes green.

Other newer solid colours include red, cream, cinnamon, caramel, and fawn.

PATTERNED COLOURS

Tortie

The sex-linked red gene will give rise to the Tortie, which is usually a female-only variety. The usual Tortie is a well-mingled mixture of red, cream and brown, with black and/or pink paw pads and nose leather and with green eyes. Torties can now be seen in several other colours including chocolate, cinnamon, caramel, and fawn; whatever the main colour, it is important for the complementary colours to be well-mingled and the eye colour to be the same as that laid down for the dominant coat colour.

ABOVE
The Oriental Cinnamon is one of the newer colours in this section, and is a warm cinnamon colour.

LEFT
The Oriental Cream should be a cool cream colour, with faint tabby markings acceptable in another good example of the breed.

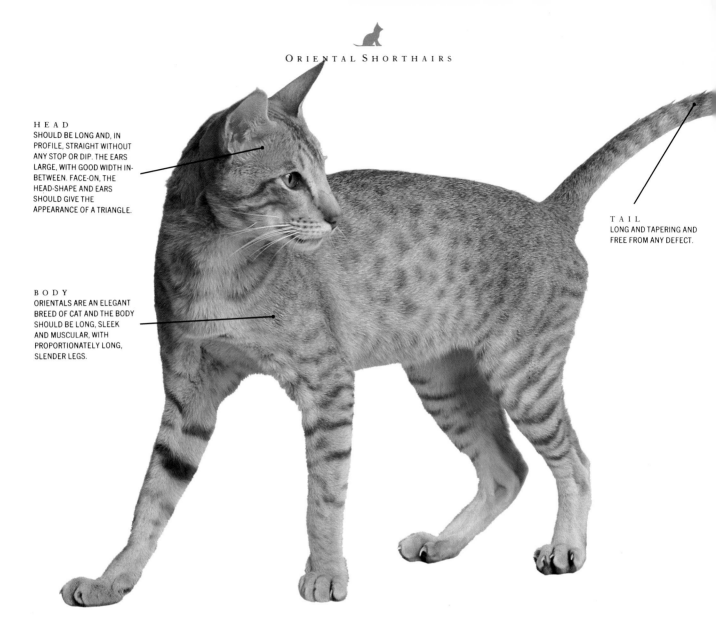

HEAD
SHOULD BE LONG AND, IN PROFILE, STRAIGHT WITHOUT ANY STOP OR DIP. THE EARS LARGE, WITH GOOD WIDTH IN-BETWEEN. FACE-ON, THE HEAD-SHAPE AND EARS SHOULD GIVE THE APPEARANCE OF A TRIANGLE.

TAIL
LONG AND TAPERING AND FREE FROM ANY DEFECT.

BODY
ORIENTALS ARE AN ELEGANT BREED OF CAT AND THE BODY SHOULD BE LONG, SLEEK AND MUSCULAR, WITH PROPORTIONATELY LONG, SLENDER LEGS.

ABOVE
An Oriental Chocolate Spotted Tabby showing good round spots that are evenly distributed.

LEFT
Whatever the colour, the Ticked Tabby should have an evenly ticked coat with two, or preferably three, bands of colour on each hair. It is acceptable for the undersides to show slight tabby markings, but the main part of the coat should be free of spots, stripes or other markings.

TICKED TABBIES

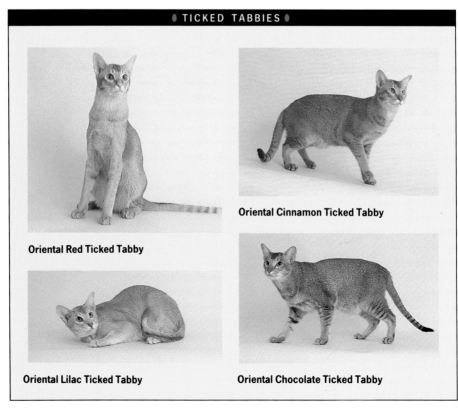

Oriental Red Ticked Tabby

Oriental Cinnamon Ticked Tabby

Oriental Lilac Ticked Tabby

Oriental Chocolate Ticked Tabby

Tabby

Tabbies are available with four different patterns: classic, spotted, mackerel and ticked. In total, Tabbies are available in more than thirty different colours. The coat and eye colour should be as laid down for the self colour.

Smokes, Shaded and Tipped

With these varieties the coat is not visibly patterned; each single hair has a different amount of colouring giving a uniform effect. In the Tipped there is only a small amount of colour visible at the tip of each hair; in the Smoke it is quite the reverse, with the coat colour extending almost to the skin. The Shaded is in-between these two. Again, it is possible to breed this series in all the colour variations.

ANGORA

T he Angora is to the Oriental what the Balinese is to the Siamese: a long-haired variety of what is usually thought of as a shorthaired breed. The fur is neither as long nor as dense as the Persian and is easier to groom. In all other respects, including character and temperament, it is essentially Oriental. Angoras can be bred in all the variations of colour and pattern acceptable for the Orientals.

● ADVANTAGES ●

● Very elegant and attractive.
● Short, close-lying coats that neither require much grooming nor shed to any great degree.
● Intelligent, affectionate and playful temperaments.
● Companionable.

● DISADVANTAGES ●

● Very loud voices, especially when calling.
● Incessant talkers.
● Can be destructive if left alone for any period of time.
● Angoras will need additional, frequent grooming.

RIGHT
The Angora is the longhaired variety of Oriental, and has a distinctive silk-like sheen to the coat. In general type and conformation, the standards are the same as the Oriental.

OTHER SHORTHAIR BREEDS

*All breeds of shorthaired cats other than British and American,
Burmese, Siamese and Oriental, are classified in the UK as
Foreign Shorthairs; for the purposes of this book, I am also
including in this section other shorthair breeds that are
available only in certain countries.*

The only characteristic these breeds all have in common is their outgoing personalities, and even so some are more demanding than others; their fur colour, patterning and texture are all completely different. These cats come from all four corners of the world, and there are many varieties. Some breeds have been imported to the West from distant countries, where they have been known for centuries – the Abyssinian, for example, thought to be a descendant of the original Egyptian cats, and the elegant Korat, the 'Si-Sawat' or sacred cat of Thailand. Then there are the naturally mutated breeds, such as the furless Sphynx, and the curly-coated Rex breeds; and also the newer, man-made 'designer' breeds, genetically manufactured by breeders, such as the Burmilla, Bengal and Ocicat.

ABYSSINIAN
(and Somali)

History

This is an old cat breed and is thought to have been imported into the UK from Abyssinia, now Ethiopia. The shape, size and distinctive coat bear a considerable resemblance to the mummified cats found in Egyptian tombs, and the wall paintings that depicted Bast and other feline gods. It is possible that the Abyssinian is directly descended from the sacred cats of Ancient Egypt, which gives a certain romance to the breed.

In recent years, a longhaired variety, known as the Somali, has been recognized. It is likely that these longhaired cats have been around for many years but, in the past, were considered to be

BELOW
The Somali is basically a longhaired Abyssinian; it conforms to the standards for this breed other than the length of fur, and is available in just as many colours.

HEAD
THE HEAD SHOULD HAVE A MODERATE, MEDIUM WEDGE AND THE MUZZLE SHOULD HAVE GENTLE CONTOURS WITHOUT BEING SHARPLY POINTED. THE EARS ARE LARGE, BROAD AT THE BASE, WIDE SET AND WITH TYPICAL EAR 'TUFTS'. THE EYES ARE LARGE AND EXPRESSIVE, WITH AN ORIENTAL SET, AND SHOULD BE AMBER, GREEN OR HAZEL.

BODY
A MEDIUM BUILD OF CAT, THAT IS FIRM AND MUSCULAR.

TAIL
FAIRLY LONG AND TAPERING, BROADER AT THE BASE THAN THE TIP; IT SHOULD NEVER BE WHIP-LIKE.

strangely coated Abyssinians. Breeders ignored their existence to the point that they would sometimes not even admit that one of these longhairs had been born to a litter of supposedly 'pure' Abyssinians. They are now, however, extremely popular worldwide.

Abyssinians have been known in the UK since the mid 1800s, when the coat colour was the ruddy brown ticked pattern known today as the 'usual' Abyssinian. Today, both Abyssinians and Somalis are bred in a variety of different coat colours, but all display the typical wild-cat ticked pattern.

Character and Temperament

Typical of most foreign breeds, Abyssinians and Somalis have highly intelligent, outgoing personalities. They do not like to be left alone, and will pine without company. Despite their wild-cat coat colouring, there is very little that is wild about their temperament; they are a very loving breed that enjoy a domestic lifestyle. However, they do not like to be overcrowded, so do not be tempted to have too many cats if an Abyssinian is your chosen variety.

LEFT
The Blue Abyssinian shows a pale oatmeal undercoat ticked with deep slate-blue.

RIGHT
The Usual Abyssinian has a golden-brown body colour, with black ticking, and the base fur should be ruddy or apricot.

BELOW
The Sorrel Somali has a coat of warm copper ticked with chocolate.

Type and Standard of Points

This should be a medium-sized cat with a close-lying ticked coat that shows a lustrous sheen. The general appearance should be of an elegant cat: the head is a round, wedge shape; the ears large and wide-set with tufted tips; the neck long, and the legs long and slender; and the tail, tapering at the tip, in proportion to the length of the body.

The eye colour should be amber, green or hazel, and the coat is now accepted in many colours: usual, sorrel, blue, chocolate, lilac, silver, fawn, red, cream, and the associated colours of tortie.

LEFT
A Sorrel Abyssinian showing the distinctive ticked coat pattern.

AMERICAN WIREHAIR AND AMERICAN CURL

History

Both these breeds are domestic short-hair varieties that display the effect of a naturally mutated gene which has only been seen in the USA to date. The American Curl has ears that curl away from the face; a misshapen ear is also seen in the Scottish Fold, but with that breed the ear flops forwards.

The American Wirehair has a unique wiry coat that is not dissimilar to that of the Cornish and Devon Rex varieties. However, the genes causing the ear shape and coat texture are quite different to those responsible for the Scottish Fold and the Rexes.

Character and Temperament

Both the Wirehair and Curl display the temperament and character associated with the other American Shorthair varieties (*see 'British and American Shorthairs'*). They are friendly, intelligent, sturdy and adaptable and make excellent pets.

Type and Standard of Points

In general, both are medium-sized breeds, with rounded heads, medium-sized, wide-set ears, and with well-developed muzzles and distinctive whisker pads. They are not as cobby or short-faced as the American or British Shorthair, and in general tend to be more elegant and graceful, similar to the general build of the Foreign Shorthairs.

ASIAN CATS
(including Burmilla)

History

This breed was the result of a modern-day Romeo and Juliet story. It was created by accident, when two lovers were barred from seeing each other. A Chinchilla male lived in the same home as a female Lilac Burmese; as youngsters, they loved to play together but when the female began to show signs of coming in to call, she was isolated in the study until she could be taken to her pre-arranged assignment with a suitable Burmese 'husband-to-be'. Unfortunately – or fortunately perhaps for the cats and the lovers of this charming new breed – the cleaner left the study door open and allowed the lovelorn Chinchilla access to his girlfriend. The resulting kittens were so instantly attractive that the owner decided that they should be given a special name, and nicknamed them 'Burmillas'.

There was no problem in finding new homes for these little cross-bred kittens; indeed, there was more interest in them than in the pure-bred Burmese kittens, and so a repeat mating was made. This was the beginning of what is now an increasingly popular breed, and explains how it gained its name.

Character and Temperament

The Burmilla is an outgoing, friendly and sociable cat that has inherited slightly modified characteristics from both of the original parents; it is not as noisy or demanding as the Burmese but is more adventurous and inquisitive than the Chinchilla. For anyone who likes the Burmese, but could not cope with the continual demands made by it, then perhaps a Burmilla is the ideal compromise.

BELOW
*Within the Asian Group are many colours of cat, the best known being the Burmilla (**RIGHT**); his litter brother (**LEFT**) is a Smoke.*

TAIL
AN ELEGANT, MEDIUM TO LONG TAIL IS REQUIRED, OF MEDIUM THICKNESS AND CARRIED PROUD.

BODY
IN GENERAL, ASIANS, LIKE BURMESE, ARE ELEGANT CATS OF MEDIUM TYPE, AND SHOULD ALWAYS HAVE A WELL-MUSCLED APPEARANCE.

HEAD
THE GENERAL STANDARD FOR THIS BREED IS FOR A CAT OF BURMESE TYPE. THE HEAD SHOULD HAVE A GOOD WIDTH BETWEEN THE EARS, AND, IN PROFILE, THE NOSE SHOULD SHOW A DISTINCT BREAK. THE EARS MAY HAVE SLIGHT EAR TUFTS IN THE SHORTHAIRED VARIETIES, WITH LONGER TUFTS IN THE TIFFANIE. FULL, EXPRESSIVE EYES SHOULD BE SET WIDE APART.

Type and Standard of Points

A breeding plan was developed to perpetuate the breed; it was decided that the Burmilla should, ideally, be a shorthaired cat of Burmese type but displaying certain traits from the Chinchilla: these included the tipped coat pattern, brick-red nose leather outlined in black, and the black markings around the eyes giving the impression that they have been outlined with mascara.

To preserve the type, the first-generation Burmillas were mated back to Burmese. This next generation gave rise to several different types of Burmilla-related cat, and at this point it was decided to use the term Asian Group to apply to all the genetic possibilities associated with this breed. This includes not just Burmillas which may be shaded or tipped, but also the self shorthair – known as a Bombay if it is Black, and an Asian if it is any other colour – the longhair version, or Tiffanie, and four varieties of Asian Tabby – Spotted, Classic, Mackerel and Ticked.

In the USA, the term Bombay refers to a Black Burmese that has resulted from a cross between a Burmese and a Black American Shorthair; the Tiffany (spelt with a 'y' not 'ie') was the result of an original cross between a Burmese and a Self Longhair.

BELOW
The Asian Ticked Tabby showing the distinctive 'M' marking on the forehead.

RIGHT
One of the original four Burmillas, the result of a mating between a love-lorn Chinchilla male and the object of his desires, a Lilac Burmese female. This was the start of a whole new group of cats.

BELOW
The Tiffanie (Tiffany in the USA) is the longhaired variety of the Asian (longhaired version of the Burmese in the USA).

BENGAL
(and Leopard Cat)

History

The spotted cat has always been highly popular, probably because the markings remind us of true wild cats. The idea of a small spotted leopard cat with the temperament of the domestic moggie seemed appealing, and so it was decided to try to breed such a cat.

In America in the early 1960s, the first planned mating took place between a domestic shorthaired cat and an Asian leopard cat, but it was not until the late 1980s that a structured breeding plan was developed. This was the beginning of the breed that we now call the Bengal. An American geneticist was particularly interested in these cross-matings, as it appeared that the Asian leopard cats did not have the feline leukaemia genome in their DNA structure, and so were immune to this virus. This made the Bengal a very sturdy breed.

As their popularity increased, they were seen on exhibition at cat shows and by 1991 were granted championship status by The Independent Cat Association (TICA) in the USA. More recently, they have been imported into the UK, where a new breeding plan has been set up.

Character and Temperament

Although a comparatively large breed, it is friendly, loving, alert, curious and intelligent. The Bengal has little fear of other cats, or any other animal, and makes a charming pet.

Type and Standard of Points

The general appearance should be of a large cat, with a coat pattern and colour mimicking that of the wild leopard cat; of equal importance is the temperament, which should be gentle and friendly. The cat should be sleek and very muscular,

LEFT
The Bengal, although popular in the USA for many years, has only recently arrived in the UK.

with the hind quarters slightly taller than the front. The coat, which should be spotted and show a distinct contrast between the spots and background colour, has an unusual texture which is more like a wild-cat's pelt than a domestic cat's fur. The head is a modified, broad, long wedge, with distinctive whisker pads, and the ears are short, medium-set and with a broad base ending in rounded tips.

BOMBAY
(see Asian Cats, including Burmilla)

BURMILLA
(see Asian Cats, including Burmilla)

BELOW
The Snow Leopard Cat is the silver version of the Bengal.

EXOTIC SHORTHAIR
(see Longhairs, Persian Type)

MANX
(see British Shorthairs)

EGYPTIAN MAU

History

The name Mau comes from the Egyptian word for cat, and the breed is basically a spotted variety of modified Siamese type. Although the GCCF in the UK used this title for many years, the breed is now referred to as the Oriental Spotted Tabby. In the USA it is still known as the Egyptian Mau where, over the years, it has developed a type quite distinct from that of the Siamese and Orientals.

Despite their glamorous name, Egyptian Maus do not come from Egypt, but have been bred for a coat pattern that resembles that of the cats in Ancient Egypt. The breed was first developed in Europe in the mid 1950s and, later that decade, was exported to the USA where it has remained popular.

Character and Temperament

As with any breed that has Siamese or Oriental ancestry, this is an outgoing, adventurous, intelligent and friendly cat that loves company and does not like to be left alone. One word of warning: as their coat pattern is so distinctive, these cats are more likely to be stolen than many other varieties and should be carefully watched if they are to be allowed outside.

Type and Standard of Points

The Mau should generally be of a modified Siamese type. The head should show a rounded wedge and, in profile, should not be as straight as the Siamese or Oriental varieties. The tail should be of medium length, tapering at the tip – not a Siamese 'whip' tail, as this is considered a fault. The eyes should be almond-shaped, neither too Oriental nor too round, and pale green. The coat is accepted in five colours: black, smoke, pewter, bronze and silver.

ABOVE
The Egyptian Mau is an American breed not dissimilar to the Oriental Spotted Tabby seen in the UK, but with less extreme Oriental type.

ABOVE

*The Japanese Bobtail,
or 'Mi-Ke' cat,
originates from Japan
and is a popular breed
in America; it is not
available in the UK.*

JAPANESE BOBTAIL

History

Not a completely tail-less variety, as some Manx, this cat shows a short 'bobbed' tail. It originates from Japan, where it is known as the 'Mi-Ke' and is considered a symbol of friendship and hospitality. The Japanese often have ceramic cats of Mi-Ke type, with one paw in the air, displayed in their homes as a symbol of welcome.

Character and Temperament

This is a most friendly breed and makes a perfect pet. It has a sweet disposition and is intelligent. It gets on very well with most other animals, and loves human company.

Type and Standard of Points

This is a medium-sized slender cat but has a feel of muscularity despite its dainty appearance. Typically, the hind legs, like on the Manx, are longer than the front legs. The tail should be carried upright when the cat is relaxed and the fur should radiate to give a similar effect to that of a well-clipped poodle. The eyes are large, oval and slanting and the head should be similar in shape to that of the Siamese, an equilateral triangle from ears to nose. Traditionally black, white and red, or tortie-and-white, many other colours and patterns are likewise accepted.

KORAT

History

The Korat is one of the oldest breeds, originating from Thailand where it was known as the sacred cat, 'Si-Sawat'. It first came to America in the early 1950s and from there arrived in the UK in 1972. The Thai name for the breed means good fortune and in their own country Korats have always been highly prized. They are a unique breed as they are only available in the original blue colour.

Character and Temperament

This is a quiet, gentle, loving breed with the sweetest of temperaments. It may seem placid, but is intelligent. It does not like loud noises or an unruly household so is best suited to a quiet home.

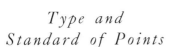
Type and Standard of Points

The most striking feature of the Korat is its sweet, heart-shaped face with lustrous round green-to-yellow eyes; the Korat's expression is quite distinctive. The head should show a gently pointed muzzle and the ears should be of medium size and set high on the head. In profile the nose should show a slight break. The coat should be short, sleek and close-lying, displaying an even silvery-blue colour all over, and, in profile, breaks in the fur along the backbone. In general, the Korat should be a medium-sized cat that is muscular and firm.

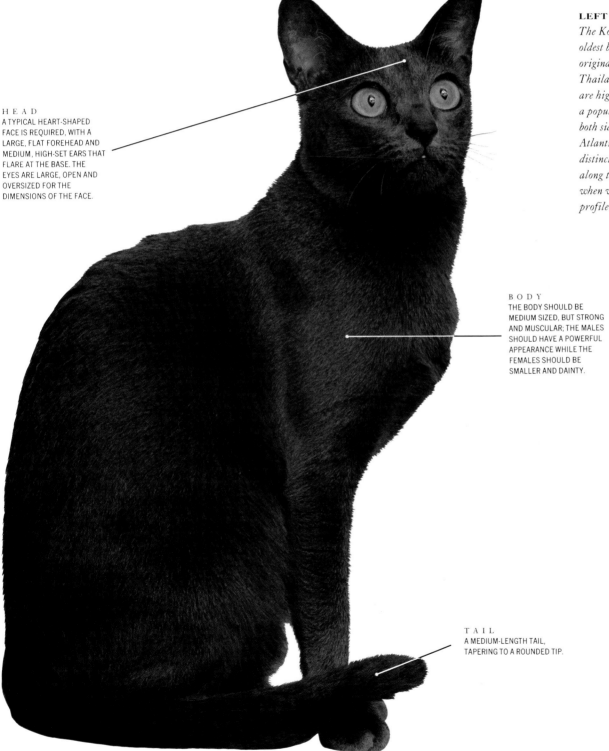

HEAD
A TYPICAL HEART-SHAPED FACE IS REQUIRED, WITH A LARGE, FLAT FOREHEAD AND MEDIUM, HIGH-SET EARS THAT FLARE AT THE BASE. THE EYES ARE LARGE, OPEN AND OVERSIZED FOR THE DIMENSIONS OF THE FACE.

LEFT
The Korat is one of the oldest breeds of cat, originating from Thailand where they are highly prized; it is a popular breed on both sides of the Atlantic, too. Note the distinctive fur breaks along the backbone when viewed in profile.

BODY
THE BODY SHOULD BE MEDIUM SIZED, BUT STRONG AND MUSCULAR; THE MALES SHOULD HAVE A POWERFUL APPEARANCE WHILE THE FEMALES SHOULD BE SMALLER AND DAINTY.

TAIL
A MEDIUM-LENGTH TAIL, TAPERING TO A ROUNDED TIP.

OCICAT

History

The Ocicat is another of the 'manufac-tured' breeds of spotted cat and is amongst the most popular; because they look rather like little ocelots, they were called 'Ocicats'.

Back in the early 1960s an American breeder was trying to develop Siamese with Abyssinian points, and so crossed a Siamese with an Abyssinian. These early litters indeed produced the pattern of Siamese desired, but they also contained assorted patterns of tabbies, including one spotted kitten who was called 'Tonga'; this little cat is generally recognized as being the first Ocicat, although he arrived as a side effect of another breed-ing programme.

Tonga was shown only once, in 1965, but by the end of that decade the breed had become increasingly popular and more and more Ocicats were being shown. Championship status was granted in America in 1987 by the Cat Fanciers Association (CFA), and they have recent-ly been imported into the UK.

Character and Temperament

This is another breed that has been gen-etically manufactured to produce what looks like a wild cat in colour and pattern of coat. In temperament and disposition, however, it is just like any other domestic cat, and is characteristically intelligent and playful – as are all the breeds men-tioned in this section.

Type and Standard of Points

The Ocicat is a moderate-type cat which should be large and well spotted. The head is a modified wedge with a broad muzzle, with just a suggestion of square-ness to the jaw. In profile there should not be a visible nose break but more a gentle rise from the bridge of the nose to the brow; the chin should be strong and the jaw firm without any sign of either being overshot or undershot. The ears are quite large and set wide apart and should never be too high or too low; ear tufts are preferable but not essential and, if pre-sent, should extend vertically from the tips of the ears. The eyes should be large

ABOVE
The typical 'wild cat' expression belies the gentle, affectionate nature of the Ocicat.

and almond-shaped, displaying a good depth of colour; blue is an unacceptable colour.

The Ocicat can be bred in ten main colours, or any of these ticked with silver. In general the cat should give the appearance of elegance but muscularity and, when held, should feel heavier than its looks suggest.

REX

History

Both the Devon and Cornish are naturally mutated breeds that first appeared in the UK in the late 1950s and early 1960s. Although they both display a curly coat, genetically they are quite different. The Cornish Rex first appeared in a litter of kittens born on a farm in Cornwall; the farmer consulted his vet about one kitten that was born with this curious coat and decided to mate it back to its mother to see what the result would be; the kittens appeared with the same strange coats. A decade later, a similar curly-coated cat was seen in Devon; this was the first Devon Rex. When two Devons were mated together they did not initially produce curly-coated offspring and from this it was realized that they were a quite distinct breed from the Cornish. The Cornish were much larger, and resembled a farm cat that had been given a permanent; the Devons were much smaller in build with large, round eyes and ears that appeared to be quite out of proportion to the size of their bodies – if they had been discovered in the 1980s, they would probably have been nick-named 'Gremlins'.

Character and Temperament

Both Rexes are a lively, intelligent and active breed. They love people and their families and adore to be included in any household activity. They can be extremely naughty – these are breeds with a pro-

BELOW
A litter of Blue-Tortie and Red Cornish Rex kittens showing the distinct curly coat.

BELOW
An adult Blue-Tortie Cornish Rex; any coat colour is acceptable for this breed.

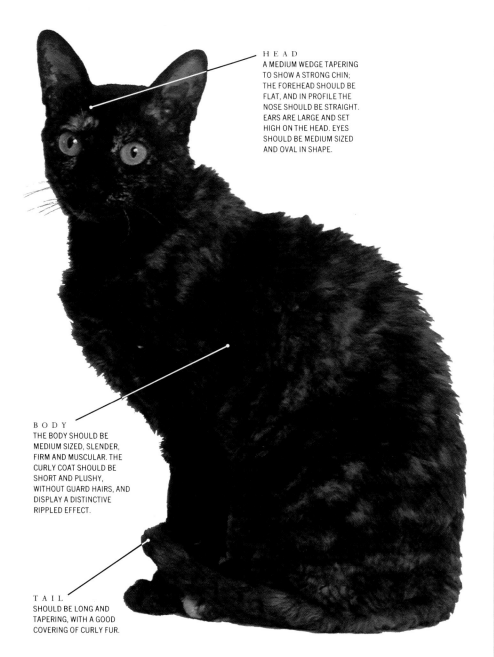

HEAD
A MEDIUM WEDGE TAPERING TO SHOW A STRONG CHIN; THE FOREHEAD SHOULD BE FLAT, AND IN PROFILE THE NOSE SHOULD BE STRAIGHT. EARS ARE LARGE AND SET HIGH ON THE HEAD. EYES SHOULD BE MEDIUM SIZED AND OVAL IN SHAPE.

BODY
THE BODY SHOULD BE MEDIUM SIZED, SLENDER, FIRM AND MUSCULAR. THE CURLY COAT SHOULD BE SHORT AND PLUSHY, WITHOUT GUARD HAIRS, AND DISPLAY A DISTINCTIVE RIPPLED EFFECT.

TAIL
SHOULD BE LONG AND TAPERING, WITH A GOOD COVERING OF CURLY FUR.

ABOVE
A Brown-Tortie Cornish Rex showing a well-rexed coat.

RIGHT
A Cornish Si-Rex, such as this Red-point, has the restricted coat pattern of the Siamese but with a rexed coat; they are available in just as many colours as the Siamese.

found sense of humour, and they are the sort of cats that you either love or hate. The Devons sometimes have less fur but neither variety has an undercoat – this means that the Rex breeds are especially suitable for people who suffer from allergies such as asthma, as there is little fur to shed.

● REX CHARACTERISTICS ●

The Tabby Cornish Rex shows paler shading on the neck, tummy and inside legs.

The main body fur should curl, giving a wave-like, rippled effect.

Even the whiskers are crinkled, which is a point required in the standards.

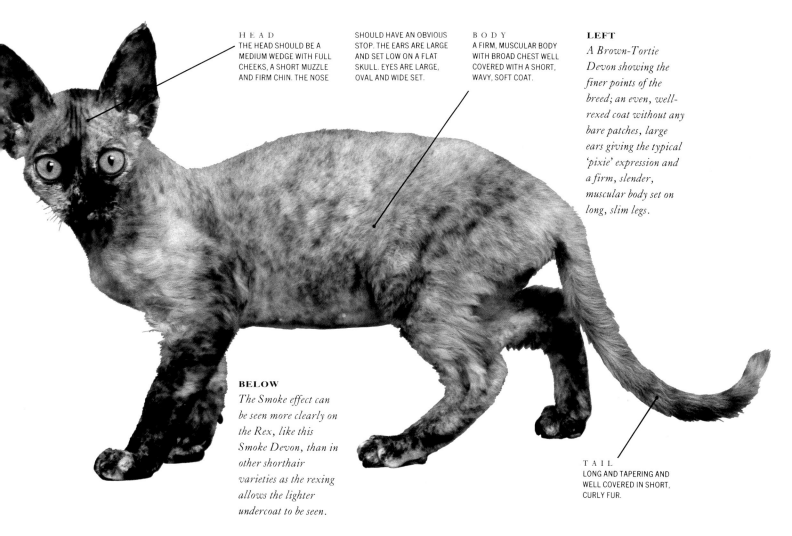

HEAD
THE HEAD SHOULD BE A MEDIUM WEDGE WITH FULL CHEEKS, A SHORT MUZZLE AND FIRM CHIN. THE NOSE SHOULD HAVE AN OBVIOUS STOP. THE EARS ARE LARGE AND SET LOW ON A FLAT SKULL. EYES ARE LARGE, OVAL AND WIDE SET.

BODY
A FIRM, MUSCULAR BODY WITH BROAD CHEST WELL COVERED WITH A SHORT, WAVY, SOFT COAT.

LEFT
A Brown-Tortie Devon showing the finer points of the breed; an even, well-rexed coat without any bare patches, large ears giving the typical 'pixie' expression and a firm, slender, muscular body set on long, slim legs.

BELOW
The Smoke effect can be seen more clearly on the Rex, like this Smoke Devon, than in other shorthair varieties as the rexing allows the lighter undercoat to be seen.

TAIL
LONG AND TAPERING AND WELL COVERED IN SHORT, CURLY FUR.

Type and Standard of Points

The Cornish should be long and elegant, but feel firm and muscular. The legs should be long, the head wedge-shaped and in profile showing a long straight nose. The eyes should be oval and the ears large and set wide apart, in a similar way to the Siamese but not so extreme. The coat should cover the body well but show distinct rexing. The Devon is altogether much smaller and does not have such profuse fur as the Cornish: it is an unusual-looking cat and not to everybody's taste. The head is round, showing a definite nose break in profile, and with distinctive large ears. As the coat is shorter than the Cornish, there are times when it can look somewhat bald. Both Devons and Cornish are available in any colour, pattern or combination of both.

RUSSIAN BLUE

History

This is another all-blue variety, but the coat colour and texture is quite different from that seen in other blue cats such as the British, Burmese and Korat. It is a cat thought to have originated from Archangel (Archangel'sk) in Russia, hence its other name, Archangel cat. Cats with similar coat colour are to be found in northern Scandinavia, so it is possible that the breed did originate in Russia and travelled to Europe by way of sailors and their ships.

Character and Temperament

Quiet, shy, loving and gentle is probably the best way to sum up the breed. Russians do not like noisy households as they are somewhat thoughtful and pensive – if they liked music, they would prefer Mozart to Wagner. They become very attached to their owners, and are quite content to be confined indoors as long as they have the company of their preferred human.

Type and Standard of Points

Russians should be medium to large-sized shorthair cats that exude elegance. They are most graceful and have been likened to ballerinas, as they appear to be walking on 'points' when they move. The fur is unusual as it is a short plush, with a typically double coat; this probably derived from the cat's need for warmth in the cold Russian winters. More recently, White Russians have appeared, but this has not been considered a worthwhile breeding programme to follow.

HEAD
THE HEAD IS A SHORT WEDGE WITH DISTINCT WHISKER PADS. THE EARS ARE LARGE AND POINTED, SET UPRIGHT; THE HEAD SHOULD BE FLAT BETWEEN THE EARS. THE EYES ARE ALMOND SHAPED AND WIDE SET.

RIGHT
The Russian Blue is an elegant cat with long, slender limbs. Although white and black Russians have been seen, there has been little interest in furthering these newer colours and the blue remains the classic example of this breed.

BODY
THE BODY IS LONG AND GRACEFUL WITH LONG LEGS; THE COAT IS QUITE DISTINCT AND SHOULD BE DOUBLE, THICK, SHORT AND SILKY.

TAIL
LONG AND TAPERING BUT IN PROPORTION TO THE BODY.

SCOTTISH FOLD

History

Although not recognized in the UK, because the deformed ears are considered an unacceptable defect detrimental to the cat's health, the breed is recognized in the USA where it is quite popular. Like the Rex varieties, the breed developed from a natural mutation and, as the name suggests, was first seen in Scotland.

Character and Temperament

Although they have a somewhat strange appearance, the Scottish Fold is a sweet, gentle breed. They are good with children, other cats and pets, and although the shape of the ear may make you suspect that these cats have problems with hearing, this has never been known to be the case.

Type and Standard of Points

In shape the cat should be of moderated British type but always showing the distinctive ears, which are folded forwards and downwards. The coat should be thick and resilient, similar to that of the Manx and other shorthair breeds that have come from the cold north. The ears should be set wide apart so that the head has a completely flat appearance. Both coat and eye colour can be of any hue.

SINGAPURA

History

This breed gained its name from Singapore where it was considered to be the 'drain' cat that lived in the gutters – which is the accepted explanation for it being smaller than most other foreign shorthairs. As Singapore is a colony containing many cat-loving 'expats', these diminutive, indigenous cats were im-mediately taken to their hearts. The slight size of the Singapura may be attributed to its deprived background, but it is generally a sturdy breed.

Character and Temperament

What it lacks in size it makes up for in character and temperament. Singapuras are sweet, loving and affectionate, although perhaps a little demure and reserved.

Type and Standard of Points

The general appearance is of a small cat that feels heavier than it looks. The ticked tabby coat looks similar to that of the Abyssinian. The ears should be large, slightly pointed and wide at the base; the eyes are large and almond-shaped and the head should be rounded, narrowing to a blunt muzzle and in profile showing a slight nose break and a firm chin and jaw line.

ABOVE
The Scottish Fold, although originating in the UK, is now almost unknown this side of the Atlantic, while it is a popular breed in America.

LEFT
The Singapura, available in Europe and America but only recently imported into the UK, originates from Singapore.

SNOWSHOE

History

Sometimes referred to as a Short-haired Birman, the Snowshoe bears no ancestry from this ancient and original breed of cat. It is, in fact, the result of mating a Siamese with an American Bi-colour Shorthair, which provided the gene necessary for the typical white pattern on the feet.

Character and Temperament

These are sweet-natured cats, displaying a modified form of the Siamese intelligence crossed with the laid-back nature of the American Shorthair – possibly the perfect combination for a pet.

Type and Standard of Points

This is quite a large breed with a short close-lying coat which may be of any colour acceptable for the Siamese or any other breed with the Himalayan factor. The eyes should always be blue, large and almond-shaped. The head should be a medium triangular wedge, in profile showing a definite nose break, but never being of Siamese type which is considered a severe fault. The muzzle and feet must be characteristically white.

SPHYNX

History

This breed is a natural mutation, first seen in Canada in 1966. Although there have been reports of hairless cats in other parts of the world, this is the only one to have been bred from, with the idea of establishing a breeding programme to perpetuate the line.

Character and Temperament

Sphynx display an outgoing character not dissimilar to that of the Rex – if you do not have much fur you have to have something going for you. This breed is certainly a conversation piece and it does not appear to suffer much from the cold, although additional heating is probably most appreciated.

Type and Standard of Points

The most important point for the Sphynx is a complete lack of fur; it is a fault for even a slight down to be perceptible. Most important is the colour, pigmentation and pattern of the skin. The body should feel hard and muscular with long, slim legs, slender neck, and long tapering tail. The head should be longer than it is wide, with a smooth profile and distinctive whisker pads.

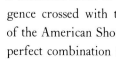

*The Tonkinese is a cross between Burmese and Siamese and is available in many colours including Blue (**RIGHT**), Lilac (**ABOVE**) and Chocolate (**BELOW**).*

TONKINESE

History

Tonkinese are basically a cross between Burmese and Siamese. They, therefore, display a little of each of these well-known breeds. They arrived by way of a breeding programme developed in North America in the late 1960s and early 1970s. Although accepted there in 1975, they are still only granted provisional status in the UK and Europe.

Character and Temperament

As with Burmese and Siamese, the Tonkinese is an outgoing, friendly and affectionate cat that will be into anything and everything.

Type and Standard of Points

In shape and size, the Tonkinese is a modified form of its original parentage; neither as long and angular as the Siamese nor as chunky as the Burmese, but a true cross between the two. Recently this breed has been given provisional status in the UK by the GCCF.

BURMESE

Although Burmese are relative newcomers to the cat fancy, they are probably one of the most popular breeds in the world today. Brown cats are reported to have existed in the Far East, particularly Thailand and Burma, hundreds of years ago; as with many travellers' tales, fact and fiction tend to get a bit muddled up. Burmese are said to have been the original 'guard cats' for the Burmese temples — but the Birman breed also lays claim to this fame too.

◆ HISTORY ◆

T he first 'Burmese' seen in the West was a small, brown female called Wong Mau, brought into America from the Far East in 1930. At this point, there was no similar male cat to mate her to and so it was decided that her beau should be a male of the breed with the closest resemblance to herself, a Seal-point Siamese. Her kittens from this litter were hybrids, close to what we now call the Tonkinese. Genetically, it is most likely that Wong Mau herself was a dark variation of a Tonkinese as when one of her sons was mated back to her, the progeny included dark brown cats like herself. These are generally regarded as the first real Burmese cats.

It was not until 1948 that Burmese found their way across the Atlantic to Britain. Burmese are not as instantly appealing, glamorous and recognizably pedigree as the Siamese; however, their intelligence and character combined with a marvellous temperament soon won them popularity. They also have the added advantage that their voices are not quite as loud as the Siamese.

As their popularity increased, and more kittens were bred, a great surprise occurred. In 1955, a silvery grey kitten appeared in a litter. It was the first Blue Burmese and was quite aptly named Sealcoat Blue Surprise. This proved that Burmese had a similar genetic make-up to Siamese: Brown Burmese is genetically equivalent to Seal-point Siamese; Blue Burmese equivalent to Blue-point Siamese. This was just the beginning. In America, a dilute version of the Brown Burmese had been noted, which was called Champagne, and a much paler version of the Blue, which was termed Platinum. These colours correspond to the Chocolate- and Lilac-point Siamese, and in the UK they are known as Chocolate and Lilac Burmese.

Once the basic genetics of the Burmese cat were understood, a whole spectrum of colour possibilities could be created. If breeders had managed to introduce the sex-linked colours to Siamese (red, cream and tortie) then why not try to produce Burmese in these colours too? A sensible breeding plan was inaugurated by several breeders, and with the help of the Burmese Cat Club in the UK to implement this programme, we now have Burmese cats in ten different colours – all of which have the health, stamina, type and temperament of the original 'Little Brown Cat', as Wong Mau was affectionately called – the little brown cat that came to the USA sixty years ago.

Burmese can now be seen in the following colours, although their titles differ in the UK and the USA: Brown (USA, Sable); Blue; Chocolate (USA, Champagne); Lilac (USA, Platinum); Red; Cream; Brown-Tortie; Blue-Tortie; Chocolate-Tortie; Lilac-Tortie. In some American cat fancies, Burmese other than Brown, Chocolate and Lilac are known as Malayans; in other fancies, the sex-linked colours are not recognized at all.

Character and Temperament

This is a quite enchanting breed, but possibly not one for the faint-hearted. The Burmese have very out-going personalities and in the past have been called the 'dog cat' due to their ability to retrieve and their loyalty to their owners. Their voices are quieter than the Siamese, but in many respects their character is similar. Burmese do not like being left alone for long without companionship, but this does not always have to be of the human variety. Another cat, or even a dog, will provide entertainment during the day if you are out at work. There is no denying that Burmese are a demanding breed – they will not tolerate being left out of the household hubbub, and they do like to be thought of as part of the family.

Type and Standard of Points

For any Burmese, the type and body shape should be the same. Burmese are a medium-sized, sturdy and well-muscled breed; they should never be as large and heavily boned as the British, nor as long and slender as the Siamese. The head should have a well-rounded dome, both in profile and front-on, with wide-set ears of medium size. The nose should show a distinct 'break', and the chin should be strong and firm. The eyes should be an almond shape and the colour, for perfection, should be any hue of chartreuse yellow, although in the UK a pale green-yellow is acceptable in an otherwise out-standing specimen. A typical Burmese conforming to these standards will have what is called the typical 'wicked' Burmese look.

The tail should be in proportion to the body length – a simple guide is that the tail should just reach the shoulder blade of the cat. It should have no visible kink or fault.

The coat should be short, close-lying, and of a clear colour. In Chocolate and Lilac Burmese it is acceptable for the points to be slightly darker, but it is preferable if the coat is of a uniform hue. In kittens, slight barring on the legs is permissible but in an adult cat this is considered a serious fault.

HEAD
THE HEAD HAS A SHORT, BLUNT WEDGE AND WIDE CHEEK BONES. IN PROFILE, THE NOSE SHOULD SHOW A DISTINCT NOSE BREAK; THE TOP OF THE HEAD SHOULD BE ROUNDED AND THE CHIN STRONG AND FIRM. THE EARS ARE MEDIUM SIZED AND SET WELL APART ON A ROUNDED DOME. EYES ARE LARGE AND LUSTROUS WITH A SLIGHT ORIENTAL SLANT.

BODY
THE MEDIUM-SIZED BODY IS FIRM AND MUSCULAR, WITH A STRONG, ROUNDED CHEST, AND SHOULD FEEL HEAVIER THAN IT LOOKS. THE LEGS ARE SLENDER AND THE HIND LEGS SLIGHTLY LONGER THAN THE FRONT LEGS.

TAIL
A MEDIUM-LENGTH TAIL, TAPERING TO A SLIGHTLY ROUNDED TIP, WITH NO FAULT OR KINK.

Coat Colours

Brown
(USA, SABLE)

Brown Burmese should show a deep, even, warm brown colour with no visible bars or stripes on an adult; faint 'ghost' markings are permissible on a kitten. The coat may shade to a slightly lighter tone on the underparts. The nose leather and paw pads should be dark brown.

Blue

A soft, silvery grey is the best way to describe the colour of a Blue Burmese, again allowing for a slight variation of shading to a lighter hue on the underparts. The paw pads and nose leather should be grey.

Chocolate
(USA, CHAMPAGNE)

Warm, milk chocolate is the colour that is called for, although the face, legs and tail can be slightly darker, but never as dark as a Brown Burmese. The nose leather and paw pads should be of a chocolate-brown colour.

OPPOSITE
The Brown Burmese is the oldest of the ten colours available, and still one of the most popular; the coat on this cat is typical for the breed and colour, and shows the correct glossy sheen.

BELOW
The required standards for Burmese differ in the USA to the UK. The American-type Burmese, as seen in this Brown, requires for a much shorter face, with rounder eyes and a generally cobbier appearance than the English counterpart.

ABOVE
A Blue Burmese youngster showing the correct soft silver-grey coat colour and silver sheen around the face and ears.

Lilac
(USA, PLATINUM)

Lilac Burmese have a most attractive colouring which should be a pale dove-grey, with a slight pinkish tinge for perfection. Like the other dilute colour, chocolate, it is acceptable for the extremities to be slightly darker. Nose leather and paw pads should be lavender-pink.

Red

'Tangerine' is the best description of the Red Burmese; however, the colour should not be too hot and certainly not so cool as to be confused with a Cream Burmese. The nose leather and paw pads should be pink.

RIGHT
An adult Red Burmese showing the correct tangerine colour.

BELOW
*The coat colour is paler in kittens and young adults, as seen in this pair of Red (**LEFT**) and Chocolate (**RIGHT**) brothers.*

RIGHT
*This adult male Lilac
Burmese shows the
correct pinky tinge to
the lilac coat and the
'jowled' look typical of
the entire male.*

LEFT
The Cream Burmese should be a rich cream colour, with a distinct 'powdering' effect around the face, ears and legs as if the cat has been lightly dusted with talcum powder.

Cream

Cream Burmese have a pale, clotted-cream colour, with a distinctive 'powdering' over their ears and heads – looking as if they have had a light sprinkling of talcum powder. Like Red Burmese their nose leather and paw pads should be a pale pink.

Brown-Tortie

For this colour a combination of brown, red and cream colours, all intermingled, is required, with the paw pads and nose leather a combination of brown or pink, or both.

Blue-Tortie

BELOW
The Blue-Tortie Burmese, showing the correct coat – a mixture of blue and cream.

Previously called the Blue-Cream, which exactly describes the colour required: a combination of blue and cream. Paw pads and nose leather should be the same, a mixture of blue and cream.

ABOVE
Tortoiseshell Burmese, such as this Brown-Tortie, are one of the most recent colours; they arrived by way of the breeding programme designed to produce Red and Cream Burmese by British breeders during the mid 1960s.

Chocolate-Tortie

The colour of the coat should be a well-mingled combination of chocolate and cream, with the nose leather and paw pads of the same colour.

Lilac-Tortie

Lilac and cream coat, with paw pads and nose leather a dove-grey.

● ADVANTAGES ●

● Very affectionate.
● Easy to groom.
● Good with children and other animals; do not object to noisy households.
● Companionable and sensitive to owners' moods and feelings.
● Playful.

● DISADVANTAGES ●

● Do not like to be left alone without a companion.
● Demanding: will want a lot of your time and attention.
● Probably the best exponents of escapology since Houdini. Keep confined if possible.
● Overtrusting so, unless trained, at risk of being stolen.

ABOVE
A Grand Champion Chocolate-Tortie Burmese showing excellent type and coat colour.

RIGHT
In profile, the Burmese head should show a distinct nose break, with a strong jaw and chin, and the top of head should show a well rounded dome; this Chocolate-Tortie sums up the standards beautifully.

SIAMESE

*The Siamese is one of the oldest breeds of pedigree cat, and over
the years many stories have been told about it, for the most part
romantic fables, but perhaps there is an element of truth in some
of them. Certainly, they add to the charm of this most exotic,
oriental and somewhat inscrutable breed.*

• HISTORY •

Of all the pedigree varieties, the Siamese is the most instantly recognizable. Long, lithe and elegant, with its distinctive darker 'points', it has always had great appeal.

Early Siamese tended to have eye squints and kinked tails, now regarded as serious faults, but with careful, selective breeding they have been mainly eliminated from the modern cat. Yet, these characteristics were once so prevalent that fables exist to this day 'explaining' how they were acquired.

It is said that Siamese cats were once sacred cats, guarding the Buddhist temples. One day, a valuable goblet went missing and a pair of the cats was dispatched to find the stolen treasure. After a long journey, the goblet was discovered and the female cat stayed to guard it while her male partner went back to tell the good news. So worried was she that the goblet might go missing again, that she wound her tail tightly around its stem and it became permanently kinked. For days and nights she sat watching over the prized goblet, never letting her eyes wander away, and by the time her partner returned, her eyes had developed a squint. Later she produced a litter of kittens – all of which had kinked tails and squints, because of her vigilance in guarding the lost treasure.

Another fable relates to a Siamese princess who, fearing that her rings would be stolen, entrusted her Siamese cat to guard them, placing them on its tail for safekeeping overnight. One night, the cat fell asleep, and all the rings fell off

*The Siamese is a long, slim and elegant cat of medium-sized build, although Siamese in the USA (**ABOVE**) have slightly different standards to those required in the UK (**LEFT**): the ears are larger and more uprightly set. However, they should exhibit, as these two Seal-point Siamese do, a pale coat colour, with well defined coloured 'points' whichever side of the Atlantic the Siamese comes from.*

her long slender tail and were lost forever. The princess decided to tie a knot in the tail to stop this ever happening again; and this could be another reason why Siamese have kinked tails.

Siamese kittens have always been highly prized. It was considered an honour for any foreigner to be presented with one of the Royal Cats of Siam, and it was an offence punishable by death for one of these cats to be stolen from the Royal Court, let alone be taken out of Siam. But, westwards they eventually came, and after many generations of selective breeding are now, along with Persian Longhairs and Burmese, among the most popular of pedigree varieties.

Siamese were originally a pale milky colour, with dark seal-coloured points on the paws, face, ears and tail. They have been known in this form for more than 200 years. In the late nineteenth century a Blue-point was recorded in the UK, but it is likely that this recessive colour had been around for some time before this. Perhaps it was not so highly regarded in Siam, and was 'swept under the carpet' as the rich Seal-point variety was more

highly prized. Over the years, dedicated breeders have worked hard to produce other colour variations in Siamese, but their names vary between the UK and North America. We now have, not only the Seal- and Blue-points, but Chocolate and Lilac (USA, Frost-point), as well as the Red-, Cream-, Tortie- and Tabby-points (USA, Colourpoint Shorthairs).

Character and Temperament

Siamese are typical of the Oriental group of cats and, like their near relations the Burmese, are a vocal breed with outgoing personalities. They are the kind of cat that you either adore or hate; they can be noisy and demanding and have a real need to be a part of the family. To aficionados, these are the plus points and they would not wish for the Siamese to be any other way. A Siamese does not like to be left on its own, so for anybody who is out at work all day, and only wants one cat, this is not the breed to select. If you want a cat that will give you life-long devotion, however, then the Siamese is for you.

Type and Standard of Points

Regardless of coat colour, the type of the cat should be the same, although standards do vary a little between those required in the UK by the GCCF and those of the various American cat fancies.

In general, the Siamese should be a medium-sized cat; long, slim, lithe and elegant, but with a definite muscular feel to it. Despite its fine bone structure (compared with the more heavily built British Shorthairs) it should be sturdy and feel much heavier than it appears. At the other end of the scale, it should never be obviously overweight to the point that it feels flabby, although some neuters can be prone to fat and a careful watch should be kept on their diet.

Looking at the cat face-on, the head should give the appearance of a triangle, topped by large, low-set, wide-spaced ears, tapering down to a pointed muzzle. In profile, the nose should be straight without any sign of a break or stop. The jaw should be firm without being either under- or over-shot. The eyes should be almond-shaped with the typical Oriental slant giving that inscrutable expression, and certainly without any trace of a squint. Whatever the coat colour, the eyes should always be of deepest sapphire-blue. The tail should be long, slender and tapering to a whip-like end; any kink or malformation is considered a serious fault. The tail should always be in proportion to the length of the cat – a rough guideline is that it should just reach the tip of the shoulder blade.

The quality, texture and the restrictive pattern of coat are what make the Siamese cat different from other shorthaired varieties. The coat should be short, sleek and fine-textured, with the fur lying close to the body. The coloured points should only be seen on the mask area of the face, the ears, legs and tail. It is considered a fault for the cat to be mismarked with lighter colours in these areas, especially around the eyes; these are commonly called 'spectacles'. Conversely, darker shading is frowned upon on the otherwise paler parts of the body.

The Siamese coat pattern is restricted to the cooler parts of the body and so, if a cat has had an operation such as spaying, it is quite likely that the post-operational shock will cause the coat to temporarily darken in that area. For the same reason, Siamese living in warmer climates tend to have paler coats than those living in cooler regions. The pointed areas should always show a uniform colour with no barring or stripes, except in the case of Tabby-points, where rings or stripes are required, and the Torties, which should show a well-mingled coat.

• COAT COLOURS •

Seal-point

A pale, even cream colour with obvious seal points restricted to the face, ears, legs and tail. The nose leather and paw pads should be a similar rich seal colour.

BELOW
The head of the Siamese, when viewed full-face, should resemble a triangle from the outward tips of the ears to the end of the muzzle.

BELOW

A Grand Champion Seal-point Siamese, showing the correct contrast of coat colour and brilliant sapphire blue eyes.

H E A D
THE HEAD SHOULD BE LONG, BUT IN PROPORTION, WITH AN ELEGANT NECK. THE PROFILE SHOULD BE STRAIGHT, WITH NO SIGN OF A BREAK OR DIP, AND THE CHIN FIRM. THE EARS SHOULD BE LARGE AND PRICKED, WIDE AT THE BASE AND SET WELL APART.

B O D Y
THE BODY SHOULD BE LONG AND SLIM YET MUSCULAR, AND THE LEGS LONG AND ELEGANT.

T A I L
THIS SHOULD BE LONG AND TAPERING, WITHOUT ANY KINK OR DEFECT.

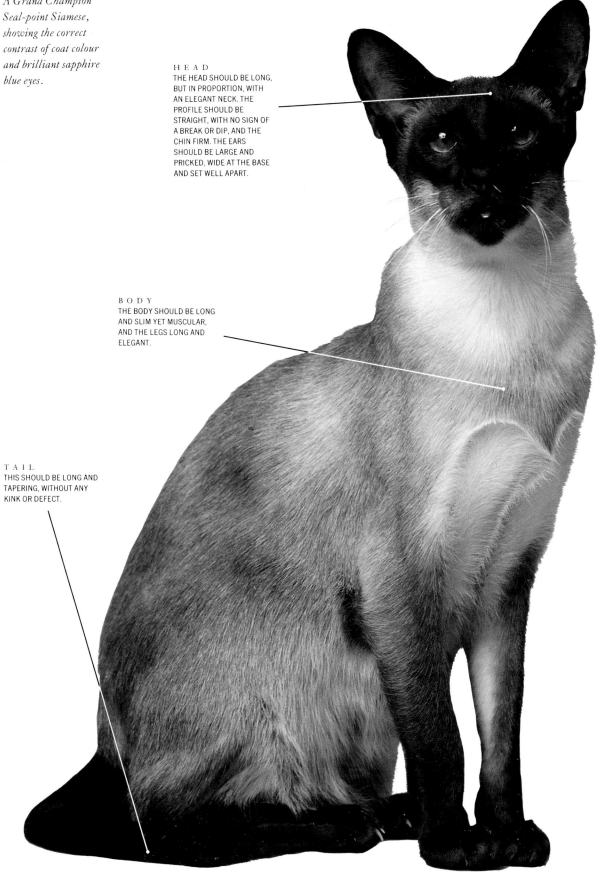

ADVANTAGES

● Highly sociable (but they do expect their owners to give them their undivided attention).
● Intelligent.
● Easy to groom.
● Give almost dog-like devotion to their owners (but tend to be 'one-person' cats).

DISADVANTAGES

● Tend to have loud voices and will use them whether or not you have invited a conversation.
● Tend to be territorial and may not get on with other, less domineering breeds such as Longhairs and British Shorthairs (they usually settle well with other Orientals and Burmese).
● Because of their obvious pedigree looks, are more likely to be stolen than many breeds.

The Siamese should always be a tall, elegant cat as well exemplified by this Blue-point (LEFT) and Lilac-point (RIGHT).

Blue-point

Cool, glacier-white is the preferred body colour, with no sign of a creamy tinge. The points should shade to a slate-blue, with nose leather and paw pads the same.

Chocolate-point

The body should be a pale ivory colour, with points, nose leather and paw pads a pale, milky chocolate colour.

Lilac-point
(USA, FROST-POINT)

Body colour should be a glacial white, with the points showing a pale, pinkish-grey tinge. The paw pads and nose leather should be lavender-pink.

ABOVE
This Blue-point Siamese has a superb head, beautiful eye colour and the correct sheen to the coat.

BELOW
The Cream-point Siamese has cream points set off against a background colour of white shading to pale cream on the back and flanks.

RIGHT
The Red-point Siamese has a white coat, shading to pale apricot on the back and flanks, with bright reddish-gold points.

Red-point
(USA, RED COLOURPOINT SHORTHAIR)

A clear white body with deep apricot-coloured points is the ideal. Nose leather and paw pads should be flesh-pink.

Cream-point
(*USA, CREAM COLOURPOINT SHORTHAIR*)

The body should be clear white, with pale, pinkish-cream points, nose leather and paw pads.

Tabby-point
(*USA, LYNX-POINT*),
Tortie-point and Tortie-Tabby-point
(*USA, TORBIE-POINT*)

These are available in a variety of colours. The body tone should be as recommended for the solid colours, with the nose leather and paw pads similar. For the Torties the colours should be well-mingled, and the Tabby-point is the only variety of Siamese that allows for stripes on the pointed areas.

RIGHT
This Tabby-point Supreme Grand Champion shows the correct long, elegant legs, good profile and coat, with clearly defined tabby markings on face, ears, legs and tail.

ABOVE
The Tortie-point Siamese, along with all Torties, is mostly a female-only variety; in the Siamese, the tortie markings should be restricted to the points only, as shown here.

ABOVE

*A Chocolate Tabby-
point Balinese
typifying the breed
with its long, silky
coat, blue eyes and
plumed tail.*

BALINESE

Balinese are, essentially, a longhaired version of the Siamese, and, in type, they should conform to the standards laid down for Siamese. Their temperament and character are slightly modified, however, probably due to the introduction of the longhair gene, so they tend to be slightly quieter and less boisterous. But the main difference is that, because they have long coats, extra grooming – and time – are required.

This longhaired variety was first seen in a litter of kittens in America. They seemed so glamorous that it was decided to breed two longhaired Siamese together to see if they bred true, which indeed they did; all the resulting kittens had long coats. The idea of a Siamese with a long, silky coat soon gained popularity, and breeders were encouraged to continue the breeding programme. By 1963, the cats were given official recognition in the USA. In the UK, things move more slowly, and it was not until the early 1980s that Balinese were granted preliminary recognition, with championship status given a few years later.

Balinese are allowed in all the colour and pattern variations that are accepted for the Siamese.

*Balinese, like Siamese cats, should display their coloured points only on the mask area of the face, the ears, legs and tail as seen in this Blue Tabby-point kitten (**LEFT**) and adult stud (**BELOW**).*

NON-PEDIGREE CATS

It is often said that the most beautiful cats at a cat show are to be found in the non-pedigree section, where cats of all different colours, patterns, coat lengths and type are to be seen. Many people take great pleasure in showing their rescued pets; these beautiful creatures have mostly had a deprived kittenhood and to see them exhibited in superb condition, healthy and with glossy coats, their pens festooned with ribbons and rosettes, gives their owners the credit they deserve.

Some non-pedigrees have a known ancestry; others may even have a pedigree parent or grandparent; the majority are waifs and strays, rescued by one of the charitable organizations, and have no known parentage. All deserve to be treated with the same love and care.

When choosing a non-pedigree cat or kitten, the same consideration should be given as when choosing a pedigree cat. Do not opt for a fluffy, longhaired variety if you do not have the time to spend on its grooming; a cat with a known part Siamese or Oriental background will be more likely to display the behaviour that is typical of these breeds – demanding cats with somewhat loud voices! With

ABOVE
This well-cared-for tortie-tabby shows beautifully rich markings.

LEFT
This exquisitely marked tortie-and-white is part pedigree. Her mother is a pedigree Oriental (father unknown) and she has inherited the affectionate and voluble characteristics typical of the Oriental breed.

BELOW
A typical, friendly 'moggie' with a pretty grey-and-white bi-colour coat.

many non-pedigrees it is impossible to know what size of cat the kitten will become; at least cats do not vary in size as dogs do, so the adult cat is unlikely to outgrow your home.

● ADVANTAGES ●

● Quite often much cheaper to buy than a pedigree or may even be given free to a good home.

● Many cat shows will offer a non-pedigree section; so if you like to participate in shows you can take your moggie along.

● Available in every possible colour, pattern and fur length.

● Generally healthy, and non-fussy eaters.

● Will give you just as much love and attention as a pedigree, possibly even more.

● DISADVANTAGES ●

● If the ancestry is unknown, you will have no indication of how your kitten will develop in terms of type, temperament and size.

● An adult cat may take some time to settle into a domestic environment.

● If severely neglected, expensive veterinary bills may arise.

SHOWING
YOUR CAT

The first formal show held especially for pedigree cats took place on 17 July, 1871. It was organized by Harrison Weir, the founder of the National Cat Club of the UK and took place at the Crystal Palace, in London. There were 160 exhibits at the event, all of which were judged to a specific standard, known then as the 'points of exhibition' (the predecessor of what we now call the 'standard of points'). Although the 'standards' required in the various breeds have changed dramatically over the years, the basic format of cat shows today still relies on Harrison Weir's ideas.

Originally, the National Cat Club was set up in the UK as an administrative body to govern and legislate all pedigree cats and their offspring. Today, the National is a cat club which still runs the largest cat show in the world, but the administration of pedigree cats in the UK is now the responsibility of the Governing Council of the Cat Fancy (GCCF).

As pedigree cats increased in popularity more cat clubs were founded and more shows organized. During World War II all such activities were put on hold and, although the GCCF picked up again, during this period some breeds came close to extinction. Fortunately, the dedication of cat lovers and breeders ensured that the breeding lines of these pedigree specimens were continued for present and future generations to enjoy.

In the 1990s, we have cat fancies in all four corners of the world, and many in between: North America, South Africa, Australia, New Zealand, Europe, South America and Singapore, to name a few. It seems almost every country has a space in its heart for the domestic cat, albeit a cat with an accredited parentage – the humble street cat is often forgotten.

Throughout the world, cat shows are run on the basic principle of judging the cat to a predefined standard. It is only the way in which the judging is arranged and the shows are organized that varies.

SHOWS IN THE UNITED KINGDOM

Most shows in the UK are run under the rules laid down by the GCCF. There are a few small shows organised by another group of fanciers, the Cat Association of Britain (CAB), which is affiliated to the Fédération Internationale Féline (FIFe), and these shows are run along European lines (*see 'European Shows'*). However, the majority of shows are run under the guidelines of the GCCF and their affiliated clubs. Shows take place throughout the year. Some are all-breed shows, organized by the region-

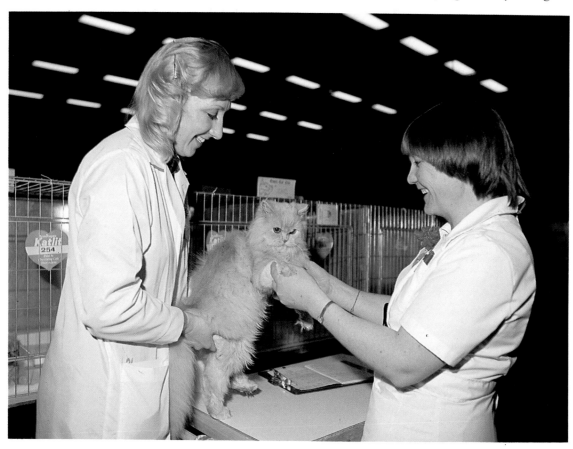

LEFT
In the UK judges go to the cats' pens to make their assessment of each exhibit; the judge is aided by a steward who pushes along the trolley, takes the cat out of the pen and generally assists the judge.

al clubs, while others are run by specific breed clubs and cater only for that particular breed. Most shows also have a non-pedigree section.

Types of Show

The GCCF licenses shows under three categories: exemption, sanction and championship.

EXEMPTION SHOWS are usually quite small affairs, often linked with a local agricultural show or similar. They are run along the lines of the GCCF, but do not have to strictly obey all the rules.

SANCTION SHOWS are like a dress rehearsal for a championship show. The classes available, the format of the show and the procedure for judging are identical to a championship show, with one exception: there are no Challenge or Premier certificates awarded, so winning exhibits cannot count any win towards the title of Champion or Premier.

There is one GCCF show that has the title of sanction, but which awards Premier certificates to the winning neuters; an anomaly it may seem, but for the simple reason that this is the annual Kensington Kitten and Neuter Cat Club Show. As there are no entire adult cats present, no Challenge certificates can be awarded, nor is it possible for a cat to be made up to Champion – so it cannot be called a championship show.

CHAMPIONSHIP SHOWS are the most popular kind as they have the bonus that the winning cats and neuters may be awarded their certificates.

Categories of Classes

There are five types of classes for pedigree exhibits: open, assessment, exhibition, miscellaneous and club (the last two commonly called the 'side' classes).

Open classes are available for all pedigree breeds, and their associated colour variations. There are separate classes for entire adults, kittens and neuter adults of each breed and colour. All adult cats have separate classes for male and female; in the case of kittens and neuters the classes may be separated by sex, depending on the number of entries. The winners of the adult and neuter classes may be awarded a Challenge certificate (entire adults) or a Premier certificate (adult neuters) if the judge feels that the overall winners are up to the prescribed standard, and are a breed with championship status. It is not unknown for such a certificate to be withheld if the exhibit is not quite up to scratch. Three such certificates, awarded by different judges, qualify the cat to use the title Champion or Premier. There are also open grand classes, which only those cats already holding the title Champion or Premier may enter; they compete within their own

group and sex (Siamese male adult, Burmese female adult, Foreign Shorthair male neuter . . .) for a coveted Grand Challenge or Grand Premier certificate. Again, three of these from three different judges qualify the cat for the title Grand Champion or Premier. All exhibits must be entered in their relevant open class, unless they are already a Champion or Premier, in which case they can opt to enter only the grand class, or both the open and the grand.

Assessment classes are for new breeds of cat to which the GCCF has awarded preliminary recognition. These are judged in the same way as the open class, but also display a provisional standard of points above their pens to help the judge assess the new breed. Those that conform to the standards will be awarded a Merit certificate.

Exhibition pens are also available at most shows and these are for cats that are not competing. Usually, exhibition pens contain cats or kittens that are of a new colour variation, or are an imported breed awaiting recognition from the GCCF. Other pens may house some famous prizewinner that the owner has decided not to put in competition any more, but which is still of great interest to fanciers. These exhibition pens are the only ones that may be decorated, and may state the name of the cats within.

The side classes are really an opportunity to get an assessment of your cats from several different judges, not just the one designated to your open class. There are various categories, such as debutante (for exhibits who have never been shown before) and limit (exhibits that have won no more than four first prizes). Your cat will also have the opportunity to compete with other types and colours of cats within its own category.

Non-pedigree exhibits have their own special section, the open classes, usually arranged by way of coat length and colour but with a special class for half-pedigree

LEFT
At GCCF shows in the UK the only decorated pens allowed are for cats that are on exhibition, and not competing; the only exception to this is the annual Supreme show where all pens are decorated.

cats. The side classes are usually more of the fun variety: classes for the cat with the largest eyes, or most expressive face — even for the one 'the judge would most like to take home'!

How to Enter a Show

The GCCF publish a list at the beginning of the show season listing all the clubs' shows, their dates, venues, the type of each show and the name and address of the show managers. Most clubs also advertise in specialist cat magazines, advising exhibitors of the date that schedules will be available and also of the closing date for entries. It is important to send off for your schedule and return the completed entry form as soon as possible; many shows have restricted space for exhibits and entries are treated on a 'first come first served' basis, with schedules being sent to club members first.

When you receive the schedule, first read through the rules carefully. Incorrect information on the entry form may disqualify your cat and any prizes won may be forfeited. Copy the name of the cat, its parents, and the registration number from your registration or transfer document. Remember that you may only show a cat if it is registered in your name.

The schedules are usually available two to three months before the show, so bear in mind that if your kitten is more than nine months old on the date of the show, it must be entered in the adult class. You may not be thinking of breeding from your cat, so it might even be a neuter by this time.

Look through the schedule, and find the open class appropriate for your breed and sex of cat; it is a common mistake to enter a neuter in the adult class, or a kitten in the neuter class. If you are in any doubt, contact your cat's breeder who should be able to advise you. Unless you are really desperate, try not to ring the show manager; he or she will be very busy sorting out all the entry forms, and will probably have family and work commitments to contend with apart from organizing the cat show.

Miscellaneous and club classes are listed, in group sections, after the open classes. Again, make sure that you are entering the right classes. For example, in the British Shorthair section there will be classes for self cats – cats of a solid coat colour; a tabby entered in such a class would be disqualified as this coat pattern belongs in the non-self classes. Check and double-check the entry form to ensure all the information is correct, and that you have entered the right classes; remember to enclose your cheque for the entry fees, too, as no entry is accepted without the appropriate amount enclosed.

Lastly, it is advisable to enclose an SAE or postcard so that the show manager can let you know that your entry has been accepted — it is not much fun to drive a couple of hundred miles with a

RIGHT

At the end of the show day, the Best in Show judging takes place and the winning cats are placed in special pens for all to admire; this cat was the best rescued non-pedigree.

● EQUIPMENT NEEDED AT THE SHOW ●

Although many shows have trade stands selling all the equipment needed for showing a cat, it is inadvisable to rely on this facility. Buy all that you will need in advance. Do not forget yourself either; most, but not all, show halls have catering facilities, so a packed lunch is often a good idea, and a folding chair as not all halls will provide adequate seating.

● The first essential is a sturdy cat carrier as no exhibit is accepted into the show hall uncontained; in the USA it is in fact acceptable, although a rarity, for cats to be confined on a collar and lead.

● In the UK all exhibits are in pens that are unmarked apart from their pen number. Each cat is allowed a plain, non-cellular blanket or piece of 'vetbed', a litter tray, water bowl and feeding dish, all of which must be plain white. In the USA, pens may be decorated and the equipment can be of any colour.

● The cats are all required to wear a tally bearing their pen number; the tally is provided, but the thin white ribbon or shirring elastic to put it on your cat is not.

● The pen that your cat will be confined to for the day has been cleaned and

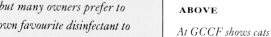

disinfected but many owners prefer to bring their own favourite disinfectant to be absolutely sure that the pen is safe.

● Do not forget cat litter and cat food – and the all-important can-opener if your cat's culinary preference is for the canned variety. Water is always available, but is often from non-mains water sources, so many exhibitors prefer to bring a small bottle of still mineral water for their cats.

● Lastly, all cats admitted to the show must have a current inoculation against FIE and, in the UK, the certificate of inoculation may need to be presented to the duty vet – so don't forget to pack the inoculation card with the show kit. Duty vets are rarely in attendance at shows in the USA.

ABOVE

At GCCF shows cats are all anonymous other than their pen number and have to be exhibited on a plain white blanket, with white litter tray and water bowl; the food bowl, seen in this pen, must be removed before the open class judging commences, as it could be construed as a distinguishing factor.

OPPOSITE

For show perfection, the coat of the British should be short, crisp and thick; many owners will allow their cats some outside access in order to crisp up the coat.

RIGHT

In most countries, cats must enter the show hall in a cat carrier. This top-of-the-range leather version may be the smartest way to travel, but any sturdy carrier would be equally suitable.

RIGHT
*In the UK, all
exhibits are examined
by a veterinary
surgeon before they are
allowed access to the
show hall.*

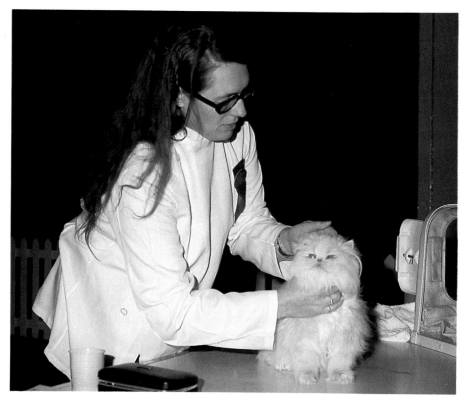

BELOW
*A Supreme Grand
Champion Cream
Colourpoint Persian,
showing the typical
long, luxuriant coat of
the breed groomed to
perfection. To be able
to present a cat, with
this length of fur, in
such perfect condition
is the result of regular,
daily grooming; it
cannot be achieved
overnight.*

howling cat in the car only to discover that your cat is not entered as the entry form did not arrive, or arrived too late.

What to Do at a Show

Cat shows start early in the day, with the doors opening for the exhibitors and their cats around 7.30 am. The owner of each exhibit will be given a tally envelope, containing the pen number of the cat, a tally showing this number, and a prize money/rosette card. Some, usually the larger, shows send this to the exhibitor a week before the event, but at others this is the first thing to be collected on arrival at the show hall.

Next is vetting-in: all exhibits must be examined by one of the appointed veterinary surgeons before entering the main hall to be penned. The vet will examine the cat for any sign of parasites, such as fleas and ear mites, fungal infections like ringworm, and any infectious disease that could be transmitted at the show. Any cat found displaying symptoms of these has the alternative of being taken back home or being kept in the isolation room.

Safely through vetting-in, you will probably be given a 'V' card to display on your pen, signifying that your cat has passed the vet's examination. Some shows ask the vet to initial your tally envelope to indicate that the cat has been examined, and this is marked off on a chart with all the pen numbers. Whichever way, it ensures that only visibly fit and healthy exhibits enter the show hall.

RIGHT
A final brush and comb before the judging commences; with longhaired breeds, it is important that all traces of talcum powder are removed from the coat as this could lead to disqualification.

The next task is to find the pen with your cat's number on it. Clean the pen with disinfectant, if you have brought it, and leave the cat to settle in with its travelling blanket, litter tray, water and perhaps some food.

When the cat has settled in, you have a little time for some last-minute grooming; if your cat is longhaired, make sure that you have brushed out all traces of talcum powder from the coat. Then place the clean, white show blanket in the pen, and remove the travelling blanket and any container of food. Also remove any toys, or anything else that could be construed as a distinguishing feature. Do not forget to put the tally around the cat's neck or, if your cat is not used to a collar, the show manager may allow the tally to be tied on the pen; remember that a cat will not be judged unless the tally is attached to either cat or pen.

At 10.00 am all exhibitors are asked to leave the hall so that the judging of the all-important open classes can begin; they are then allowed back into the hall usually between noon and 12.30 pm.

As soon as the hall is cleared of exhibitors, the show catalogue will be available to all except the judges and their stewards. From this, you will be able to see exactly what competition your cat is facing and how many are in the various classes that you have entered.

The open class results will start coming up between 11.30 and noon, and as these are the most important classes there will be quite a crowd around the results board. The results slips are placed in numerical order of class, so are easy to locate. The slips themselves show only the pen number of the cat, again in numerical order, with the award number written at the side. This goes in order: 1, 2, 3, R (reserve or fourth), and the winners receive a rosette (some shows only award rosettes to the first three placings) and a prize card. In large classes of top-quality cats the judge may award further prizes of VHC (Very Highly Commended), HC (Highly Commended) and C (Commended) and the exhibit will be awarded a card to this effect.

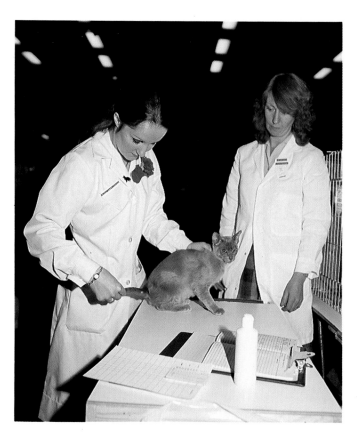

ABOVE

In all tailed breeds of cat, the judge will examine the cat's tail to ensure that it is free from a fault or kink.

The winning male and female cats in the three opens (adult, kitten and neuter) for each particular breed and colour are then judged against each other for the Best of Breed rosette. Adults and neuters not entered in the open class, but only in the grand class, can also be considered for this award.

If the winning cat is up to the standards laid down, the result slip will indicate 'CC' (Challenge certificate) or 'PC' (Premier certificate) after the number 1; 'CC W/H' or 'PC W/H' shows that the judge has declined to award the certificate. It is possible that if the standard is too low the judge will withhold the first prize altogether, and '1 W/H' signifies this decision. 'CNH' against a pen number denotes the cat could not be handled. The rosettes and prize cards are then put on the pens in due course, but not until all the open class judging has been completed.

The side classes are judged after the opens; some shows will offer a choice between prize money and rosettes, although most these days seem to just give rosettes. If there is a choice, you have to take your prize card to the rosette table in order to claim your preferred award.

At the end of the day some shows will hold a Best in Show competition ending up with the best adult, kitten and neuter in each of the seven sections and, if there is a non-pedigree section, a Best in Show Non-pedigree too. There are also cups available for club members to hold for one year; some shows will give them out on the day of the show, while others present these trophies at their annual general meetings.

SHOWS IN OTHER COUNTRIES

Throughout the world, the main objective of any cat show is to find the best example of each particular breed on the day of the show. These winning cats go on to win appropriate certificates that eventually afford them their respective championship status. The main differences between the UK and the rest of world lie in the way the shows are organized, the methods of judging, the recognized breeds eligible to enter championship classes, and the titles given to the winning cats. Also, British shows do not use the ring judging system and the pens are undecorated so that the cats have complete anonymity. Show preparation, schedules and entry forms, catalogues and the necessary equipment remain pretty much the same in whichever part of the world you show your cat.

American Shows

There are many governing bodies in the USA, all with different rules and regulations; some recognize certain breeds and colour patterns, and others do not. However, the main bodies are the Cat Fanciers Association (CFA) and The Independent Cat Association (TICA). Ring judging is the method used, so the cats'

❖ HOW THE JUDGES WORK ❖

In the UK the judge, accompanied by a steward, goes to the cat's pen; the steward is provided with a trolley so that the cat can be examined both in and out of the pen. The steward is also responsible for handling the cat and presenting it to the judge for his, or her, decision. In the USA and Europe, where ring judging is the main system, the steward's duties also include collecting each cat from its pen and delivering it to the judge in the appointed ring. The only time this happens in the UK is at the annual Supreme Cat Show, where a system of ring judging is also employed; the cats are brought to the judge, and the owners and members of the public are allowed to watch the judging. Because the judge never goes to the cats' pens these are allowed to be decorated, and any previous awards displayed for all to admire. To qualify to enter the Supreme, a cat has to already be a full Champion or Premier, or have gained at least one certificate in the previous show season; in the case of kittens, a win at a championship show secures entry. The highlight of the day is the final judging for the three Supreme winners: adult, kitten and neuter.

Pedigree cats are judged to the standards laid down for their particular breed and colour, but the condition, temperament, general health and presentation of the cat are also taken into consideration. If two cats are of similar quality, but one is groomed better, displays a sweeter disposition or even simply has a cleaner show blanket, this may well be reflected in the judge's placing of the exhibit. In the case of non-pedigree cats, where no 'standard of points' exists, these are the main criteria for the judging placements – along with a little subjective viewing on the part of the judge who may well prefer a tortie to a tabby!

BELOW
The judge will need to assess the eye colour of each exhibit, and here the steward is holding the cat so the judge can look at the cat closely.

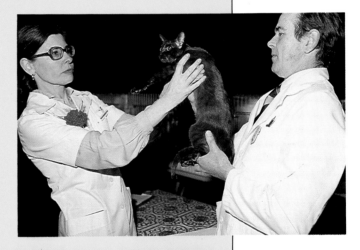

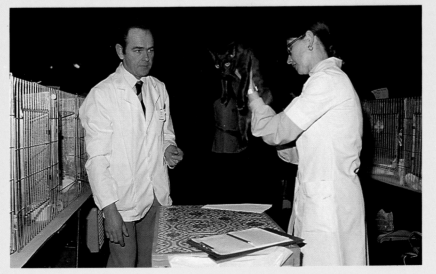

LEFT
Having assessed the finer points of the breed, the judge will wish to hold the cat in order to assess the weight, condition and general conformation of the cat.

● DIFFERENCES BETWEEN SHOWS IN UK, USA AND EUROPE ●	UK (GCCF)	USA (general)	EUROPE (FIFe)
Exhibit to be registered in exhibitor's name	✓	✓	✓
Active/non-active register	✓	"NOT FOR BREEDING" MAY BE MARKED ON "BLUE SLIP"	✗
Vetting In	✓	✗	✓
Exhibits have to have been inoculated	✓	✓	FIFe REQUIRE INOCULATION AGAINST BOTH FIE & CAT FLU
Production of inoculation certificate	✓	✗	✗
Exhibits to be taken to show in carrier	✓	✗	✓
White show equipment needed	✓	✗	✗
Decorated pens allowed	ONLY AT SUPREME	✓	✓
Ring judging system	ONLY AT SUPREME	✓	✓
Pen judging system	✓	✗	✗
Open classes available	✓	✓	✓
Miscellaneous classes available	✓	✗	✗
CC, CAC, CACIB . . . certificates awarded	✓	✗	✓
Conferring of Champion/Premier title (3 shows/3 different judges)	✓	✗	✓
Can be made up to Champion at one show	✗	✓	✗
Judge's written report available on show day	ONLY AT SUPREME	✓	✓
Judge's written report published in specialist journal	✓	✗	✓
Cats/kittens may be purchased direct from show	✗	✓	✓

BELOW
In Europe, as in America, the pens are allowed to be decorated, as the judging takes place in a separate ring away from the area where the cats are penned.

pens can be highly decorated. The judging is an event that exhibitors and members of the public alike can sit and watch, with the judge giving a running commentary on the assessment of each exhibit. Unlike UK shows, a cat is entered in its breed class only. Under the CFA rules, a cat can become a Champion in a single show, and if the main judge thinks the cat of sufficient merit, two other judges will be asked to confirm the opinion and the award will be made.

Australian Shows

Shows in Australia are run very much in the same way as in Britain, with the judge going to the cat and not vice versa, and the pens are undecorated. The Australians are currently looking into the practicalities of ring judging but, for the present, abide by the GCCF system that the Co-ordinating Cat Council of Australia (CCCofA) has opted for.

European Shows

Clubs in Europe are mainly governed by the Fédération Internationale Féline (FIFe), the largest governing body on the Continent. Any shows run by FIFe-affiliated clubs have to abide by their rules in much the same way as the GCCF administers the rules of cat shows in Britain. Shows are all judged by the ring judging method, so the pens are usually highly decorated.

Cats are exhibited in the hope of winning a *Certificat d'Aptitude de Championnat* (CAC), the equivalent of the GCCF's Challenge certificate, or for those already made up to champions, a *Certificat d'Aptitude de Championnat International de Beauté* (CACIB), which is of the same status as the Grand Challenge certificate. Winning three certificates from three different judges, just as in the UK, entitles the cat to use the title Champion or, in the case of a CACIB, International Champion. There is no restriction on livestock being moved within European countries, and this title (the equivalent of Grand Champion in the UK) seems most suitable, as the most worthy of this honour have been shown in more than one country.

FIFe and the GCCF have considerable liaison, and it is quite common for British judges to adjudicate at Continental shows, and for FIFe judges to judge at the shows in the UK – the standard of points are all the same.

● THE JUDGES' REPORTS ●

The whole object of taking your cat to a show is to get an honest appraisal from the judges, so this is the single most important part of the whole day. All judges' reports in the UK are published in the weekly magazine Cats, *and the monthly magazine* Cat World *publishes a* Show World *section listing the winning cats, but without the judges' comments. It may be possible to talk to your judge during the show, but never interrupt a judge while he or she is still judging or your cat may be disqualified. (On receipt of an SAE, most judges are happy to send a copy of their report to you after the show.)*

The exception to this is the annual Supreme Show, and assessment classes in other shows, where the judges leave a written appraisal of each exhibit on the pen.

At FIFe shows, the judges provide a written report on the show day, and in America competitors have the best of both worlds – a running commentary while the judging is being carried out as well as a written score sheet itemizing how the points were awarded.

USEFUL ADDRESSES

A list of the official organisations of the major international cat fancies, together with their official or semi-official journals.

AUSTRALIA

Co-ordinating Cat Council of Australia (CCCofA)
Box No 4317 GPO
Sydney
NSW 2001

Council of Federated Cat Clubs of Queensland
c/o Secretary
June E Lobwein
19 Clifford St
Toowoomba 4350

Feline Association of South Australia
c/o Secretary
Mr Lee Caldwell
21 Poole St
Osborne 5015

Feline Control Council of Queensland
c/o Secretary
Mrs A Barrett
84 Anzac Ave
Redcliffe 4020

Feline Control Council of Victoria (RAS)
c/o Secretary
Mrs Marion Jones
Royal Showground
Epsom Road
Ascot Vale 3032

Governing Council of the Cat Fancy in Victoria
c/o Secretary
Mrs Sandra Weaver-Hall
PO Box 73
Oakleigh 3166

Murray Valley Cat Authority
c/o Secretary
Miss Shirley E Osmond
PO Box 406
Mildura 3500

Queensland Independent Cat Council
c/o Secretary
Miss Pat Mercer
PO Box 41
Esk 4312

RNCAS Cat Club
c/o Mr Bjorn Christie-Johnston
PO Box 404
Dickson 2602

JOURNAL

Royal Agricultural Society Cat Control Journal
Box No 4317 GPO
Sydney
NSW 2001

EUROPE

Fédération Internationale Féline (FIFe)
c/o Secretary
Mme R van Haeringen
23 Doerhavelaan
Eindhoven 5644 BB
Netherlands

JOURNAL

A Tout Chat
(service des abonnements – subscriptions)
BP 205
Versailles 78003
France

SOUTH AFRICA

Governing Council of the Associated Cat Clubs of South Africa
c/o Mrs M Simpson
45 Edison Drive
Meadowridge 7800

All Breeds Cat Club
PO Box 1078
Cape Town 8000

Cat Fanciers' Club of South Africa
PO Box 783100
Sandton 2146

Eastern Province Cat Club
PO Box 5166
Walmer 6065

Natal Cat Club
100 Marian Hill Road
Ashley
Pinetown 3610

Rand Cat Club
PO Box 180
Springs 1560

Transvaal Cat Society
PO Box 13385
Northmead 1511

Western Province Cat Club
PO Box 3600
Cape Town 8000

UNITED KINGDOM

Governing Council of the Cat Fancy (GCCF)
4–6 Penel Orlieu
Bridgewater
Somerset TA6 3PG

GCCF Cat Welfare Liaison Committee
c/o Secretary
Mrs Barbara Harrington
79 Pilgrim's Way
Kemsing
Near Sevenoaks
Kent TB15 6TD

Feline Advisory Bureau
350 Upper Richmond Road
Putney
London SW15 6TL

JOURNALS

Cats
5 James Leigh St
Manchester M1 6EX

Cat World
10 Western Road
Shoreham-by-Sea
West Sussex BN4 5WD

UNITED STATES

American Cat Association (ACA)
8101 Katherine Drive
Panorama City
CA 91402

American Cat Fanciers' Association (ACFA)
PO Box 203
Point Lookout
MO 65726

Cat Fanciers' Association (CFA Inc)
PO Box 1005
Manasquan
NJ 087361005

Cat Fanciers' Federation (CFF)
9509 Montgomery Road
Cinncinatti
OH 45242

The Independent Cat Association (TICA)
PO Box 2988
Harlingen
TX 87550

JOURNALS

Cat Fancy
PO Box 4030
San Clemente
CA 92672

Cats
445 Merrimac Drive
Port Orange
FL 32019

Cat World
PO Box 35635
Phoenix
AZ 850969

INDEX

ACKNOWLEDGEMENTS

My most grateful thanks to my editor LESLEY ELLIS who has helped to make this book much more readable.

ROY ROBINSON F.I.BIOL. who advised me on genetics and checked related text.

My veterinary surgeon, JOHN OLIVER B.VET.MED., MRCVS, for his advice and help in ensuring the veterinary facts are as up to date and accurate as possible.

SUE KEMPSTER (British), SALLY FRANKLIN (Orientals), DAVID FROUD (Maine Coons), ANGELA SIVYER (Manx) and ALAN WATTS (Norwegian Forest Cats) for their help in providing suitable cats of their respective breeds for photography.

LESLEY PRING and the staff of the GCCF for their advice on cat breeds.

MARJORIE HORNETT for allowing me to photograph her Bengal and Ocicat, and for the valuable information she provided on these breeds.

LARRY JOHNSON, for supplying photographs of American breeds that do not yet exist in the UK.

DAPHNE NEGUS for her advice on the Pan-American aspects of the Cat Fancy.

ROSEMARY ALGER for reading through the manuscript to check for any omissions.

LYNDA TAYLOR and the LYNCHARD CHINCHILLAS.

COLOUR CENTRE (LONDON) LTD for processing transparencies with their usual care and efficiency.

MIRANDA VON KIRCHBERG for valuable information on the Burmilla/Asian breeding programme.

Lastly, my grateful thanks to my friend LYNN VAN HAEFTEN who has kindly done my shopping, errand running and kept me supplied with everything I needed while writing this book!

● CREDITS ●

Photographs by Paddy Cutts, Animals Unlimited. The publishers and author would like to thank the following for additional picture material: Larry Johnson, pages 9 *t*, 39 *b*, 48 *tl*, 49 *c*, 55, 70, 71, 75, 76, 83 *t*, 91 *b*, 101; Murray Thomas, back jacket flap; Edward Young, pages 116, 118 *t*.